Pioneers *of* Religious Renewal

Pioneers *of* Religious Renewal

A History of The Christian Community
in the English-Speaking World

Christian Maclean

Floris Books
1976 – 2016

First published in 2016 by Floris Books

© 2016 Floris Books
All rights reserved. No part of this book may be reproduced in any form without permission of Floris Books, Edinburgh
www.florisbooks.co.uk

British Library CIP Data available
ISBN 978-178250-315-6
Printed in Great Britain by Bell & Bain Ltd

Contents

Foreword *by Christward Kröner*	7
Preface	9
1. Beginnings of The Christian Community	13
Initial approaches and first courses with Steiner	22
The Autumn Course	31
Preparations for the founding	32
The founding	38
First steps	53
2. Beginnings in Britain	65
First visits	66
Permanent step to Great Britain	67
Growth in London	82
3. Wartime and Postwar Years	89
First years of the war	90
The Christian Community on the Continent	92
Middle and end of the war	93
The immediate postwar	103
Albrighton Hall and Woodford House	110
The fifties	113
London	117
Camphill and The Christian Community	120
The sixties and seventies	121
Shalesbrook	127
Ireland	130
Consolidation	132
The Christian Community Press and Floris Books	135
An overview today	136

4. Expansion to America — 138
First visits — 138
Adam Bittleston's visit — 139
The first American priest — 143
Prague — 144
Beginnings in New York — 145
The East Coast — 149
Chicago — 152
Canada — 163
The West — 164
Stegmann's 'American Action' — 166
Translation — 169
South America — 173

5. Southern Africa — 175
First visits — 175
The Cape — 179
Johannesburg — 184
Natal — 190
Translating the rituals into Afrikaans — 191
Namibia — 193

6. Australia and New Zealand — 194
First visits — 194
Founding — 199
New priests — 203
Sydney's disaster — 203
The present situation — 204
The Philippines — 205

7. Conclusion — 207

Appendix — 209
The 48 founding priests — 209

Chronology — 231
Notes — 234
Bibliography — 237
Index — 239

Foreword

In this convincing book Christian Maclean gives an overview of the development of The Christian Community in the English-speaking world, using his detailed knowledge of a wealth of individual biographies.

With his quiet sense of humour and succinct implications, the author encourages readers to complete the full picture of events using their own imagination. He successfully sketches the threads connecting the lives that led to the founding and growth of this movement for religious renewal in different countries and congregations. Again and again, we are shown the pioneering spirit and the willingness to take on poverty and suffering displayed by those who developed this movement.

It is valuable that the author not only relates the positive and joyful events, but also shows some of the shadow sides and difficulties connected with the growth of The Christian Community, especially where priests could not work together, or where finances went awry.

In the Preface the author rightly states that his book only shows one side of the whole – for he concentrates essentially only on the working of priests. A history of the friends and members should be written one day. For without them no congregation could exist, nor could The Christian Community fulfil its task.

One of these members is the author himself who once studied at the seminary, and, without becoming a priest, has contributed to the health and wellbeing of this movement over the last forty years.

I am pleased that this book exists. I value it as a precise source that, while focusing on the past, helps to open the way to the future, and I trust it will find interested readers.

Christward Kröner
Berlin, May 2016

Preface

The Christian Community is a new church born in the present age, recognising individual people's freedom to discover their own truths independently of any imposed doctrinal dogmas. Priests wear vestments and the sacraments are celebrated, but in a renewed form in a language of today. Priests undertake to celebrate these sacraments objectively, without personal alterations or additions.

This book traces the development of this movement from its beginnings in Germany and Switzerland, and then how it spread into English-speaking countries. It is written for those who know The Christian Community, and so it does not go into its teaching or sacraments. They need to be experienced to gain a feeling and insight into what this movement for religious renewal really is.

I must also make an apology straight away, for the very name 'The Christian Community' indicates congregations of priests *and* members. This book only tells half the story, for almost all the people described and mentioned here are priests, but without members and friends the priests cannot fulfil their task. Historically, though, it is perhaps right, for the beginnings of this movement were driven by priests. It is only in relatively recent years that communities and congregations have formed independently and then asked for a priest to join them – Australia and New Zealand, and to some extent South Africa, have shown this pattern.

Inevitably I have made choices, selected which events to describe, of which figures to include a short biography. Other people would have made other selections and highlighted other aspects; like any history, it is to some extent subjective. Another question of course is where to stop. In each chapter I have concentrated on the beginnings, for they are most distant and there are fewer people still alive who remember the events or people involved. I have quoted anecdotes, for they often bring figures to life. I have then tried to give an overview of the present situation, but I am aware of the, often large, gap between the beginnings and the present day. Other people may take up the task of filling those gaps.

I have included some of the failures within The Christian Community, those who did not keep their vow to serve as a priest for the rest of their life. In some earlier descriptions details have been glossed over or were too close and painful to mention. But I felt the idealism and light of the movement was more clearly illustrated when the disappointments and shadows were also shown.

Some of the terminology used should perhaps be explained for those unfamiliar with it. The Eucharist or communion service is called the Act of Consecration of Man.

There is an administrative hierarchy of office holders known as lenker, oberlenker and erzoberlenker. The hierarchy does not have different degrees of ordination, nor is it meant in terms of a pyramidal organisational structure, but more as having an overview and coordinating function. A lenker (from the German *lenken*, to steer or guide) is responsible for a region – at present there are four such English-speaking regions: Britain and Ireland, North America, Southern Africa and Australasia. The oberlenkers (usually two) together with the erzoberlenker (the head of the Community) form the international leadership, which is often augmented by a further four lenkers to form the Circle of Seven. It is the Circle of Seven that 'sends' priests to their congregations; priests do not simply choose by themselves where they might like to work. There are so many priests' moves described in this book – technically almost all of them 'sendings' – but for brevity this is implied.

Some of the historic references are to the time when The Christian Community was banned in Germany by the Nazi authorities from 1941 to the end of the war. For brevity I have simply called this time the *Verbot*.

PREFACE

Alfred Heidenreich wrote a stirring account of the beginnings of The Christian Community, *Growing Point,* and one of my early tasks at Floris Books was to update it for a new edition published in 1979 for the fiftieth anniversary of the Community in Britain. Now, almost forty years later, it is still an excellent book, but cannot simply be updated, so I have freely quoted from it.

I am also most grateful for the help I have received from Rudolf Gädeke who wrote (in German) about the 48 founders of The Christian Community. I have made extensive use of his book, quoting, paraphrasing and summarising. His brother Wolfgang, with whom he worked setting up the Community's archive in Berlin, has been particularly helpful in answering a string of obscure questions and often giving a wealth of anecdotes about past events. Janine Jenitschonok at the archive in Berlin has been unbelievably quick and diligent at laying her hands on documents and photographs.

Michael Heidenreich, Alfred Heidenreich and Marta Heimeran's son, has also been extremely helpful and encouraging in this project, digging out old papers and filling gaps in my understanding. When I was confirmed, Alfred Heidenreich recommended reading an obscure book if unable to go to sleep, adding, 'I can recommend any one of mine.' Three years later, when staying in Berlin with his son, and unable to sleep, I spotted *Growing Point* on his shelf, and so started reading it ... around 4:30 in the morning as the birds were beginning to sing I had finished that riveting account.

I would also like to thank the many people who have read certain chapters and made suggestions: in Britain Roger Druitt; for North America Oliver Steinrueck and James Hindes, and Richard Lewis who collected everything he could on the Community's history in North America; for Southern Africa Neville Adams, Reingard Knausenberger and Peter van Breda; for Australia and New Zealand John Shaw and Cheryl Nekvapil. My apologies to all the others whom I have not mentioned by name.

The photographs have been collected from a great number of sources, and it has been impossible in most cases to identify who originally took them.

1.
Beginnings of The Christian Community

In the wake of the First World War, many young people in Germany were searching for something new: new values, a new social or political order, a new outlook and purpose in life, new forms of religion. The old order had collapsed and the country was in turmoil. The Communist uprisings of 1919 in some cities and the subsequent nationalist counters are often forgotten.

Students searched for answers at university, but many were disappointed. In *Growing Point*, Alfred Heidenreich (one of the founding priests of The Christian Community) described his own situation, having studied at three different universities over two years:

> But gradually I sensed that my profound disappointment with university life had another cause. I had accepted the universities unquestioningly as the sources of learning which offered the key to the mastery of life. But I became aware that this had been an illusion. It might be that the universities still held the key to jobs in the Establishment. But had not the Establishment miserably and ignominiously collapsed all round? Instinctively I realised that the traditional academic approach to the world had a great deal to do with the 'decline of the West', of which it was fashionable to speak. It dawned on me that the German universities – 'the intellectual bodyguard of the Hohenzollern' as they had proudly called themselves – were in a large measure the intellectual fathers of a way of life which had been discredited by the verdict of history. I could not have put it so bluntly or precisely at the time. But [fundamentally] this is what I felt, and this was the cause of my malaise.[1]

Some of these students, including Heidenreich, found their way to anthroposophy and the great thinker Rudolf Steiner, who gave them profound answers to their quest. In the first years of the twentieth century Steiner, out of his insights into the spiritual world, had written and lectured to a few intimate groups in different cities. But towards the end of the First World War greater numbers of people heard him speak, and practical activities gained from anthroposophy, his science of the spirit, had been emerging. Steiner responded to requests to help in a wide range of different realms: the Waldorf School in Stuttgart was started because Emil Molt, the owner of the Waldorf Cigarette Factory, wanted a school for his employees' children; other endeavours – in medicine, agriculture and education for special needs – later came about with Steiner's help.

It would be out of place to try and give a comprehensive picture of Steiner's life and work in the context of this book, but Alfred Heidenreich, gave some impressions of him:

> Steiner was and remained in a class by himself. There simply wasn't anybody one could compare him with. He was truly extraordinary. Quiet, humble, dignified, immensely alert, he touched every subject with the unassuming assurance of a master and the originality of genius. In a word: in him the evolution of human consciousness had reached a new stage. While we ordinary mortals sit in the Platonic cave with our backs to reality painfully deciphering the shadows cast against the inner wall, Steiner achieved the spiritual feat of turning round. Eventually he saw reality face to face.[2]

From 1916 onwards Rudolf Steiner hinted at a renewal of religion, but not as a task of anthroposophy itself. In a lecture of 1917 he stated:

> It should never be claimed that our attempts at spiritual science are a substitute for the life and exercise of religion. Spiritual science may be taken as a support, as a foundation for the life and exercise of religion in the highest sense, and particularly in relation to the mystery of the Christ, but it should not be made

Rudolf Steiner

into a religion. We should be clear that religion in its living form and practice kindles the spiritual consciousness of the human community.

If this spiritual consciousness is to become a living thing in human beings, we cannot possibly remain at a standstill, settling merely for abstract ideas of God or Christ, we must stand renewed amid the religious practices and activities (which may take different forms in various people) as something that provides people with a religious centre and appeals to them as such.[3]

One of those who heard this lecture was Friedrich Rittelmeyer, who at that time was probably the best-known and most prominent preacher and religious writer in Germany. Rittelmeyer was a follower of Steiner.

In 1911, at the time when Rittelmeyer met Steiner, he had a far greater following in Germany than Steiner. Rittelmeyer could fill not only the biggest churches, but the biggest lecture halls. His followers numbered thousands, while in those days Rudolf Steiner's following numbered barely hundreds. It is to Rittelmeyer's lasting honour that he recognised, in spite of external appearances, the unique greatness of Rudolf Steiner's spiritual stature.[4]

In a conversation, Steiner told Rittelmeyer that he (Steiner) had to confine himself to science of the spirit, but that religion was Rittelmeyer's task. Despite this and despite Rittelmeyer's quest for new forms of liturgy, he did not ask Steiner any more about his thoughts on religious renewal, and it took another three years before others did.

Friedrich Rittelmeyer in 1935

Friedrich Rittelmeyer
1872 October 5, Dillingen, Bavaria – 1938 March 23, Hamburg

Born into a Lutheran pastor's family as the oldest of seven children, Friedrich Rittelmeyer was a lonely boy, without friends, with frail health and a melancholic temperament. However, he was gifted and hard-working and was always top of the class at school. He read all the German classics and went on to read the *Iliad* and the *Odyssey* in Greek before he was fourteen.

At the death of his sister he experienced an angel, a glimpse into another world. He was always certain he wanted to be a minister of God, despite his misgivings about the teachings of the Lutheran Church and its emphasis on sinfulness.

He studied theology in Erlangen and Berlin, graduating top of his class of fifty. But he felt unsatisfied: 'I had theology, but no religion, no Christianity.' In his search for meaning, on reading Carlyle's *Sartor Resartus* he experienced something of the eternal. This experience was reinforced when in Berlin, in the Neue Kirche where he would later preach, he heard the 100th Psalm set to Mendelssohn's music. Following this he had the inner certainty to become a minister, and took up a trainee post in Würzburg where he also completed his doctoral thesis. He used to spend up to 25 hours preparing a sermon, but this seems to have borne fruit, as people felt they had real substance.

In 1902, after passing his final exam with an excellent result, he applied for positions in Vienna, Rome, London and Berlin, but was finally only offered the position of third preacher at a church in Nürnberg, where he gave weekday afternoon sermons. In 1904 he married Julia Kerler, and over the years they had six children.

In Nürnberg he got to know Christian Geyer, who had arrived there at the same time to be the main preacher at St Sebald's. They soon became firm friends, together battling for a more liberal theology in the rather orthodox Bavarian Lutheran church. Together

1. THE BEGINNINGS OF THE CHRISTIAN COMMUNITY

Friedrich Rittelmeyer and Christian Geyer

they published a volume of their sermons in 1904, and from 1910 they edited the journal *Christentum und Gegenwart.*

Rittelmeyer continued his own writing, lecturing and preaching and was soon recognised far beyond Nürnberg as a profound and reverent thinker. As a student he had planned to write a book on Jesus by the age of forty, and this he duly did: *Jesus* was published in 1912.

In 1910 he was asked to give a lecture about modern religious movements, and characteristically thorough, he found the Theosophical Society (this was prior to the breaking away and founding of the Anthroposophical Society) about whose teaching he knew nothing. He read books and met Michael Bauer, the local leader of the society. Over the next few years he made a thorough study of anthroposophy, heard Steiner lecture, and soon had meetings with him. He describes his careful, almost sceptical approach to and final embrace of anthroposophy in *Rudolf Steiner Enters My Life*. Once convinced, he openly acknowledged and supported Steiner (by the beginning of the First World War Rittelmeyer was probably the most famous Lutheran preacher in Germany, and much more widely known than Steiner). This support culminated in 1921 when he wrote and edited tributes to Steiner for his sixtieth birthday (*Vom Lebenswerk Rudolf Steiners*), which became the most influential book on anthroposophy, given the standing of its editor.

In 1916 Rittelmeyer was asked to be the main preacher at the Neue Kirche in Berlin, colloquially known as the German Cathedral. Several theological students met regularly with Rittelmeyer in Berlin to study anthroposophy, including Bock, Kurras, Adolf Müller, Gitzke and Franke.

Despite both great men's clear recognition that a new approach to religion was necessary and that a new form of liturgy was needed, it remains a mystery why Rittelmeyer never asked Steiner more. Steiner was always willing to help where others had questions and requests, but he did not see it as his own task to take the initiave. It fell to others to approach Steiner, which led to the June and Autumn Courses in 1921 and ultimately to the founding of The Christian Community. Rittelmeyer, who at that time was on extended sick leave following a climbing accident, was kept informed of the events by Bock. Some of the younger ones who took part in these initial courses only met Rittelmeyer in late 1921, as Heidenreich describes:

> I remember very well his first appearance in our circle in Berlin ...
> I must confess that for me it was something of a shock.
> Of course I was deeply interested and in a very real sense already committed to this coming movement for religious renewal.
> But anything even faintly parsonic or reminiscent of religion in the usual style sent cold shivers down my spine. It was inevitable that at that first meeting with us Rittelmeyer should still show something of the exterior of the Lutheran parson. Later on he transformed this in the most exemplary and moving manner. But for the moment some of us had to swallow hard.[5]

It was soon after studying and meditating on the text of the Act of Consecration of Man in September 1921 that Rittelmeyer decided to work for this new movement:

1. THE BEGINNINGS OF THE CHRISTIAN COMMUNITY

It dawned on me that here was the possibility of creating a divine service in which all true Christians could be united, which could be regarded as the central point of a truly Christian communal life, around which a new, manifold, ever-growing religious life unfolds. Slowly it was borne in upon me: this must not be withheld from humankind! You yourself dare not fail now if you do not want to transgress against humanity and the divine revelation! And if it is impossible to bring this to people in the existing forms of the church, then something new must be ventured![6]

He resigned his prominent position in the Lutheran Church in June 1922. Heidenreich commented, 'His letter of resignation was not even acknowledged. The ecclesiastic authorities did not write a single line of thanks or regret to the man who had given the church a quarter of a century of historic service.'[7] He spent the following few months preparing for his new task together with Geyer and Bock.

After the founding, Rittelmeyer and his family moved to Stuttgart, as he wanted to be closer to the German centre of Steiner's work, and Steiner asked Rittelmeyer to be on the board of the German Anthroposophical Society, a task he conscientiously carried out until he resigned in 1933 when the Anthroposophical Society split.

In The Christian Community Rittelmeyer saw himself as brother among brother-priests and preferred not to take on a leading role. However, Steiner persuaded him of the necessity of having one leader, not as the top of a pyramid-like hierarchy, but as a central focal point. In February 1925 Rittelmeyer was installed as erzoberlenker. A few weeks later Rudolf Steiner died, and Rittelmeyer held his funeral.

From the beginning, Rittelmeyer edited the monthly journal, for the first year called *Tatchristentum* (Christianity of deeds) and from 1924 *Die Christengemeinschaft* (The Christian Community), as well as writing books – at least one every year. Reading his writing today, some of the language and approaches seem dated, but there are still gems to be gleaned. *Rudolf Steiner Enters My Life* and *Meditation* are both still bought and read today. Rittelmeyer also travelled and lectured widely, especially at the many big conferences that took place in those early years.

The 1930s brought their share of difficulties and disappointments. Two of the leading priests, Johannes Werner Klein and Gertrud Spörri, broke their commitment to the movement and left, and in Germany the rise of the Nazis led to the banning of the Anthroposophical Society in 1935 and the suppression of Waldorf schools. In the late 1930s the existence of The Christian Community was also threatened, and Rittelmeyer was involved in negotiations with the authorities to ensure its continuance.

Throughout his life Rittelmeyer suffered from a frail constitution and a melancholic temperament, but his spirit radiated trust in the divine world. The great father figure of the movement for religious renewal died while visiting Hamburg in 1938.[8]

Initial approaches and first courses with Steiner

In 1920 three students, Johannes Werner Klein, Gertrud Spörri and Hermann Heisler, each independently asked Steiner about a new direction for Christianity in the light of anthroposophy. He gave encouragement and was willing to help, but it was only in May 1921, when the three students met at a conference in Stuttgart and shared their views with other students, that they realised the full potential of Steiner's responses. They put together a request, which one of them, Gottfried Husemann, formulated as a memorandum to Steiner on behalf of a number of young students.

Hermann Heisler   *Gertrud Spörri*   *Johannes Werner Klein*

The memorandum presented to Rudolf Steiner

In demselben Sinne haben eine Erklärung abgegeben:

Robert Spörri, cand. theol. Zürich
Wilhelm Cloormann, cand. theol. Mannheim
Ludwig Nonnenmacher, stud. theol. Mannheim
Walter Gradenwitz, stud. theol. Wiesbaden
Martin Borchart, stud. phil. et theol. Marburg
Rudolf Meyer, Hamburg
Richard Gitzke, stud. theol. Berlin
Otto Franke, stud. theol. Berlin
Horst Münzer, stud. phil. et theol. Berlin
Emil Bock, cand. theol. Charlottenburg
Eberhard Kurras, cand. theol. Saaleck (Hüning.)
Ernst Uhlauff, stud. philos. Breslau
Otto Becker, Hauslehrer, Holzminden

Es fehlen noch einige Unterschriften.

The memorandum presented to Rudolf Steiner

1. THE BEGINNINGS OF THE CHRISTIAN COMMUNITY

We, the undersigned, are convinced that the unfolding of spirit-consciousness is what humanity today is wanting above all to achieve; and we are convinced moreover that 'religion in its vital life, in its living practice within the social life enkindles spirit-consciousness'. These two facts seem to us to indicate a direction for the activity that we have perhaps to undertake from within the anthroposophical movement.

We are only able in this present time to approach the idea of priesthood – priesthood as connected with the practice of religion – with a certain caution and reserve, so long as on the one hand it is derived only from such priestly and clerical institutions as have existed hitherto; and inasmuch as on the other hand we do not know whether something like priesthood has to be at all, or whether something else must be put in its place. Finally it is our belief that all further questions concerning what has been described as religious practice and religious activity, or concerning the religious milieu that ought to form the environment of human life from birth to death, can only rightly be put when his first question has been dealt with. We therefore now ask Dr Steiner to give us information on this matter.

From the answer, each one of us will see for himself whether he is able to undertake a task in this connection or not.

Stuttgart, May 22, 1921.
Werner Klein
Gertrud Spörri
Ludwig Köhler
Gottfried Husemann
(The following names were also listed on the reverse: Robert Spörri, Wilhelm Clormann, Ludwig Nonnenmacher, Walter Gradenwitz, Martin Borchart, Rudolf Meyer, Richard Gitzke, Otto Franke, Horst Münzer, Emil Bock, Eberhard Kurras, Ernst Umlauff, Otto Becher)

Heidenreich described what followed:

Rudolf Steiner responded at once. He invited the two representatives who had handed him the letter to an interview ... [He] made sure of the sincerity and strength of their impulse, and being satisfied, promised an early meeting of several days, with lectures and discussions in which he would explain what should be done. 'About all these matters one must speak at length,' he said. The promised meeting, which took place from June 12–16, 1921, grew to the size of a full course. From the beginning it far, far surpassed all expectations. Rudolf Steiner revealed his power from a new angle. He showed himself as a complete master of all things which belong to the life of a church. Ritual, priesthood, pastoral care, organisation and finance, social tasks and responsibilities, everything was touched upon with unmatched originality and fullness. Many revolutionary points were put forward with complete matter-of-factness. The movement should form free [independent] congregations, women were to work on a basis of complete equality with men, the sacramental mysteries of Christianity were to be renewed.[9]

Hermann Heisler, who had been excluded to begin with because the young students did not want anyone over the age of thirty to be involved, was hastily invited to the course following Steiner's intervention. As far as possible the religion teachers from the Waldorf School took part (Herbert Hahn, Wilhelm Ruhtenberg, Paul Baumann, Ernst Uehli and Leonore von Mirbach). Lehofer, a stenographer, recorded the lectures and two discussion sessions. Marie Steiner was also present.

It was agreed that everything would need to be described and discussed more thoroughly in a larger circle in the autumn. Rudolf Steiner invited this circle – he hoped for ten times more than the initial twenty – to the Goetheanum at Dornach. There would be friends there who could help with the initial finances, and Heisler took on the difficult task of raising necessary funds.

1. THE BEGINNINGS OF THE CHRISTIAN COMMUNITY

The small group was fired with enthusiasm and made arrangements for a multitude of tasks to find people who might be prepared to join this work:

Gertrud Spörri travelled to Dornach to organise finances, accommodation and meals for a three-week course. In Berlin, Emil Bock formed a central point for exchange of information. Together with Eberhard Kurras, Johannes Werner Klein, Rudolf Frieling and Gertrud Spörri, he produced an information brochure about this new movement. Gottfried Husemann did the same, consulting with Steiner ... Friedrich Rittelmeyer, who could not take part in the June Course because of his health, wrote a flyer: 'Foundations for the Work of Religious Renewal'. The shorthand notes from the initial course were transcribed and duplicated, to be sent to those who had taken part and to those who might take up this task. Hermann Heisler started to raise funds, which was initially difficult, but surprisingly successful.[10]

Emil Bock
1895 May 19, Barmen (Wuppertal) – 1959 December 6, Stuttgart

Bock was a quiet and shy but gifted boy. He grew up in a simple textile worker's family; Ernst Wahl, his father's boss, a philanthropic liberal Jew, helped to send him to secondary school. His father died when Bock was only sixteen, but the boss continued to support him as he went on to study modern languages in Bonn. Though his parents were not churchgoers they sent him to Sunday school; this was his only religious background. At the end of the first semester of study the First World War broke out and Bock volunteered. After three weeks in Flanders a ricochet shot hit him in the back leaving a fist-sized wound, and he was left for dead in no man's land. He recalls being out of his body, hovering above, and seeing a burial detachment arrive after thirty hours. He summoned all his willpower

Emil Bock in 1916

to shout out: the faint whimper was heard and he was taken to a field hospital where he made a slow recovery. This experience gave Bock a certainty of the spiritual world, which sustained him for the rest of his life.

After six months in hospital he was sent to Berlin where he studied Latin, Greek, Hebrew and theology while working as a part-time postal censor (on account of his knowledge of French and English). There he noticed a steady stream of packages to Switzerland containing books by Rudolf Steiner. He began to take them home overnight to read. On August 20, 1916, he was wandering back from early Sunday morning duties when he came across a great number of people surging towards the Neue Kirche and decided to follow them. It was Rittelmeyer's inaugural sermon in Berlin. This made a deep impression on Bock, and soon afterwards he met Rittelmeyer. Gradually over a number of meetings Rittelmeyer spoke with Bock about anthroposophy, and took him to some lectures by Steiner.

Now, aged 21, Bock began an intensive study of anthroposophy. He completed his theological studies and became a minister in

1. THE BEGINNINGS OF THE CHRISTIAN COMMUNITY

Berlin. He had started a theological student group with Rittelmeyer, which Kurras, Müller and Gitzke joined. Despite their deepening anthroposophical studies they had not yet envisioned a greater task ahead. Only at the end of April 1921, when Spörri visited Bock and told him Steiner had offered to hold a course for theologians, did Bock wake up to the potential. From that moment onwards, Bock was not only fully behind the new movement, but a driving force that pushed the founding circle relentlessly forward. He was often the mediator between the older and younger members of the group, between those who wanted time to prepare thoroughly (like Rittelmeyer) and those who took Steiner's words literally: 'There's no time to lose.'

After the founding of The Christian Community, Bock went to Stuttgart with Rittelmeyer, Spörri and Beckh. He travelled continually, supporting lone priests in their congregations, lecturing and speaking at conferences. In November 1922, on one of his lecture tours, he married Grete Seumer, who he had known since his youth in Barmen. They had four children, but Bock was away so much that the children experienced him only as an occasional visitor.

Despite his many duties, he found time to study new subjects and travel more widely. He explored every place he visited thoroughly, seeing its history come alive before his eyes. And he wrote ceaselessly – almost every month there was an article in the German journal, and over the years a growing number of books appeared. After a trip to Italy he wrote *The Catacombs*, which appeared in 1930 in German (and the following year in English as the first illustrated book from the infant publishing venture of the British Christian Community). From reading his books and the many authors he quotes, one might gain the impression that Bock had a large library. But he possessed few books and relied on his extraordinary memory.[11]

Of all his travels, the two visits to the Holy Land in the 1930s probably made the deepest impression on him. The guide who showed his group around often found that Bock would take over, most memorably at Ein Gedi on the Dead Sea where Bock, out of mysterious depths of intuition, described Essene communities living in this part of the Judean Desert.¹² It was not until 1947 when the scrolls were found at Qumran that Bock's intuition was confirmed by archeological excavations. His knowledge and insights of the land inform his great series of books about the Old and New Testament. In the books on the Old Testament that were published during the time of the Nazi regime and growing anti-Semitism, Bock courageously showed a deep appreciation of Jewish history and culture.

In 1938 Rittelmeyer died unexpectedly. Bock, his appointed successor, now felt the full weight of responsibilities for the young movement. Since 1935 the Anthroposophical Society had been banned in Germany, and the same fate threatened The Christian Community. Recurring negotiations with government departments allowed the Community to continue without compromising its principles until 1941, when despite all efforts it was banned. Most of the priests were arrested and imprisoned for a short time, a few for longer; Bock was held in a concentration camp for eight months. His colleagues were haunted by a double fear: either he would be executed, or he would die of malnutrition and from the war wound in his back. Even Bock admits he lost his characteristic certainty in this time. However, he survived, and after his release he got an office job in a friend's firm, which allowed him considerable free time. This enabled him to keep contacts alive and organise an astonishing degree of underground activity.

Towards the end of the war most churches and chapels were destroyed in bombing raids. In Stuttgart the seminary was largely destroyed by a heavy delay-action bomb, and in October 1944, during a night of terror, the Urachhaus (residence of several Christian Community priests and of the publishing activity) as well as the big Community house containing the church and hall were destroyed. Bock managed to save his house in the Ameisenberg Strasse by lifting the incendiary bomb that had penetrated the roof and throwing it into the garden.

Immediately after the capitulation of Germany he sought out colleagues and members, many dispersed or lost in the chaos of that time. Bock found a hall that became a makeshift chapel and worked

1. THE BEGINNINGS OF THE CHRISTIAN COMMUNITY

again tirelessly in rebuilding The Christian Community, not only in Stuttgart but right across Germany.

The fourteen years from the end of the war to Bock's death were a time of expansion of the movement, both in Germany and in other countries. He died in December 1959 aged 64. Typical of his tireless activity, his last words were a rather surprised, 'Is it time already?'

In his books Bock often shows great archetypal patterns. His own life falls into three archetypal 21-year phases with clear turning points. He began studying anthroposophy aged 21. This was followed by the founding period of The Christian Community, which lasted just over 21 years. Aged 43, he became erzoberlenker after Rittelmeyer's death, and for the last 21 years of his life he shouldered the difficult time of suppression and destruction then rebuilding and expansion.[13]

The Autumn Course

The target of 'ten times' the twenty attendees of the June Course was not reached for the Autumn Course, but a circle of 120 assembled at the Goetheanum in September 1921.

The first Goetheanum at Dornach

> But the composition of the audience was less homogeneous than it had been in the spring. In the endeavour to reach the required number, people had been invited whose unconditional preparedness was not equal to that of the original group. In particular, a number of ministers were admitted whose interest stopped short at a theological discussion. This presented a difficulty...
> After this course something like a hiatus occurred. Most of the fellow-travellers dropped away and the young generation was occupied with the digestion of much spiritual material which was new. In those weeks and months Rudolf Steiner stood by. He did not take any initiative; he never did in matters in which initiative had to come from others. But when a move was made to recapture the original impetus he was again immediately ready to give practical advice.[14]

Friedrich Rittelmeyer, who was unable to take part in the course owing to illness, had been kept informed by Emil Bock, and by the end of 1921 resolved to join this new movement. This was tremendously important and put the whole enterprise on a firmer footing. Rittelmeyer's close friend and well-known preacher, Christian Geyer (1862–1929), also joined those preparing for this new religious movement.

Preparations for the founding

Despite Rittelmeyer and Geyer taking this important step, the path towards the founding was still unclear. In January 1922 three of the younger future founders, Heisler, Borchart and Klein, met Steiner, who suggested that those still interested should write a memorandum affirming their wish to found this new movement for religious renewal. This apparently arbitrary action caused some friction with Rittelmeyer and Bock in Berlin, who felt more thorough preparation was needed.

During a student course that Steiner gave in Berlin in March 1922, most of the founders were present, and Rittelmeyer met the

1. THE BEGINNINGS OF THE CHRISTIAN COMMUNITY

whole circle for the first time. Some harsh disagreements surfaced between those feeling the urgency of the task (mainly the younger ones) and those who wanted more time to prepare. The matter was only resolved by Steiner meeting the group and advising them not to lose any more time. He asked each member in which city they were going to start a congregation over the following months.

Now things began to move faster. The founders went to different cities of Germany to lay the foundations of 'free, independent congregations'. Rittelmeyer resigned from his position in the Lutheran Church in June 1922. In June and July, Rittelmeyer, Christian Geyer and Emil Bock, who were expected to become the leaders of the movement, were invited by Count and Countess Keyserlingk to Koberwitz, where two years later Steiner held his Agricultural Course. There they prepared for preliminary meetings with Steiner in Dornach that took place in July and August.

From August 16 to September 4 the founders gathered at Breitbrunn on the shores of the Ammersee at the foot of the Bavarian Alps.

Margarete Morgenstern's house in Breitbrunn, Bavaria

Michael Bauer (1871–1929)

One of the true saints of the anthroposophical movement lived at Breitbrunn, Michael Bauer, who was one of the most intimate disciples of Rudolf Steiner and an intimate friend of the poet Christian Morgenstern. He lived now in retirement. Frau Margarete Morgenstern, the widow of the poet, took care of him. He spoke very little, but it was an experience to see him walk through his little orchard. He seemed a personal friend of all his trees, which confided in him and communed with him ... Frau Morgenstern and he, as far as his strength allowed, had made the preparations for our stay.[15]

It came as a tremendous blow to Rittelmeyer and some of the others when, just as they had gathered at Breitbrunn, Christian Geyer withdrew. Coming from a long line of Lutheran ministers, the sacramental rituals with vestments, which were central to the new movement, felt alien to him, despite his deep appreciation of the insights into Christianity that came from Steiner.

The interior of the stable at Breitbrunn where the founding group met

Our meeting place was an empty byre, with a vaulted ceiling and real windows. The built-in feeding troughs were filled with straw and served as seats, supplemented by a collection of chairs kindly lent by the local peasants. In the centre a table was improvised with a few rough boards. Decorated with green branches and a few prints, the byre made a cool and friendly assembly hall quite suitable for a gathering of new poverellos...

There we met day after day for two weeks, read the text of the Act of Consecration of Man which we had no authority yet to celebrate, treated each other to little addresses and discussions, and nursed our plans and wishful thoughts for the future. The difference of our age levels was strikingly obvious; it seemed also to go through each one of us individually. Rudolf von Koschützki has described what he felt when he first appeared in our circle. 'I found myself in a curious dilemma. When I looked at a speaker, I said to myself: this is a student; but when I closed my eyes I had to say to myself: this is a professor, not an imitation but a real one, who speaks with expert knowledge and modesty. I have never

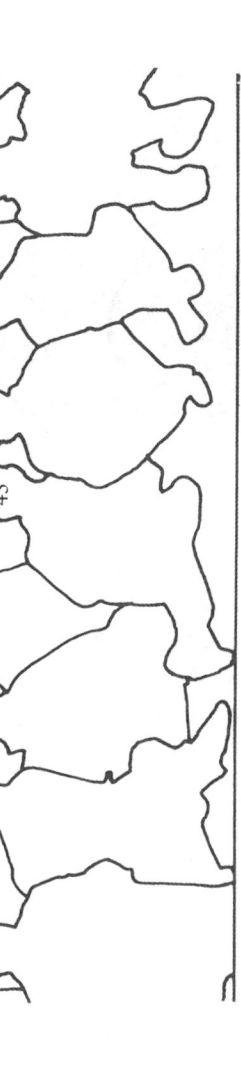

The founding priests gathered at Breitbrunn in August 1922.
1. Johannes Perthel (1888–1944); 2. Hermann Beckh (1875–1937); 3. Wolfgang Schickler (1894–1960); 4. Adolf Müller (1895–1967); 5. Wilhelm Kelber (1901–67); 6. Gustav Spiegel (1900–1977) 7. Carl Stegmann (1897–1996); 8. Marta Heimeran (1895–1965); 9. Martin Borchart (1894–1971); 10. Friedrich Doldinger (1897–1973); 11. Rudolf Frieling (1901–86); 12. Waldemaar Mickisch (1900–1944); 13. Kurt Willmann (1902–2003); 14. Kurt Philippi (1892–1955); 15. August Pauli (1869–1959); 16. Eberhard Kurras (1897–1981); 17. Hermann Fackler (1886–1978); 18. Wilhelm Ruhtenberg (1888–1954); 19. Heinrich Ogilvie (1893–1988); 20. Alfred Heidenreich (1898–1969); 21. Rudolf von Koschützki (1866–1954); 22. Arnold Goebel (1897–1972); 23. Fritz Blattmann (1882–1969); 24. Joachim Sydow (1899–1949); 25. Jutta Frentzel (1901–99); 26. Gertrud Spörri (1894–1968); 27. Heinrich Rittelmeyer (1879–1960); 28. Rudolf Koehler (1899–1992); 29. Karl Ludwig (ordained in 1923, 1892–1931); 30. Otto Becher (1891–1954); 31. Gottfried Husemann (1900–1972); 32. Friedrich Rittelmeyer (1872–1938); 33. Claus von der Decken (1888–1977); 34. Wilhelm Salewski (1889–1950); 35. Ludwig Köhler (1900–1985); 36. Harald Schilling (1902–43); 37. Eduard Lenz (1901–45); 38. Gerhard Klein (1902–80); 39. Rudolf Meyer (ordained later in 1922, 1896–1985); 40. Kurt von Wistinghausen (1901–86); 41. Richard Gitzke (1896–1989); 42. Otto Franke (1897–1956); 43. Johannes Werner Klein (1898–1984); 44. Walter Gradenwitz (1898–1960); 45. Emil Bock (1895–1959); 46. Thomas Kändler (1901–57); 47. Hirschberg ? (not ordained); 48. Erwin Lang (1897–1985); 49. Paul Balke (not ordained).

*Rudolf von Koschützki,
the oldest of the founders, in 1934*

met such a curious assembly in my life.' From the vantage point of his 56 years Koschützki could observe what we younger ones certainly were not conscious of. But for the record let it be said that during the rest of the day we were anything but professors. Fiddle, flute and guitar took over in the evening, and the lake echoed with our songs.[16]

On September 5, 1922 the final number of 45 founders crossed the lake at sunrise in little boats to catch the early train that would bring them to Dornach.

The founding

There was a great difference between the Dornach meeting of 1922 and the Autumn Course that had been held there the previous year. Until the 1922 meeting some things were tentative – the new movement did not even have a name.

1. THE BEGINNINGS OF THE CHRISTIAN COMMUNITY

From the first moment Rudolf Steiner took everything into his own hands, and the foundation events proceeded apace. At the first meeting he told us that we should all leave Dornach different men from what we were when we came, and that we should all be ordained. He gave the name 'The Christian Community' *(Die Christengemeinschaft)* to the new Movement. 'The name must be simple and challenging,' he said. He also gave the name to the new communion service: 'The Act of Consecration of Man' *(Die Menschenweihehandlung)*. All this was given with the greatest naturalness in a few sentences...

A vow was taken, and the community of the founder circle established. Under Rudolf Steiner's close personal guidance a body of seven office holders was established [Heidenreich was the youngest of these]. Now the preparations went ahead for the first celebration of the Act of Consecration of Man. Rudolf Steiner repeatedly read and demonstrated every detail. He gave the patterns for the priestly vestments, and the three members of the founder circle who were to become the first women priests in Christian history took the making of them in hand...

During the first Act of Consecration of Man, which now began and which proceeded in stages through several days, Friedrich Rittelmeyer received his ordination through Rudolf Steiner. He thus became the first Christian priest in the new dispensation. Through Rittelmeyer the ordination was then enacted and passed on to the rest of us...

On September 16, 1922 the first celebration of the Act of Consecration of Man was completed and we have since counted this day as the birthday of The Christian Community.[17]

The ordination service is interwoven within the Act of Consecration, and at that first ordination on that day 25 priests were ordained. The remaining twenty were ordained the following day.

Apart from Rudolf Steiner and the founders themselves, only Marie Steiner, Albert Steffen and Ernst Uehli were present during the foundation events. Steffen wrote in his diary:

*Albert Steffen (1884–1963) was present at
the first Act of Consecration of Man*

Today the first Act of Consecration of Man was completed on the earth out of the spirit, and at which the Risen Christ was present ... I can say that Christ was there, for when the words of bread and wine were spoken I saw his resurrected light-life-body. It is the first time that I have seen the being of Christ. His arms were outstretched and there was a radiance about his head. And I experienced then that he healed and hallowed. He was there, and is there.[18]

Rudolf Steiner's role in the founding of The Christian Community was not that of founder, but of helper and guide. Alfred Heidenreich 'with great reserve and respect' offered a comparison:

During the critical forty years in the wilderness, when the small fragments of the Hebrew nation were forged into the bearer of a divine promise for all mankind, Moses, the man of God, brought down from the heights of Mount Sinai the word of God for God's purpose at the time. In this process Moses was guided to establish the Levitical priesthood. But Moses did not himself assume the priestly office and function. He ordained his brother Aaron as the fountainhead of the new priesthood.

Had we witnessed and were we involved in a similar event in our time? To the pedestrian mentality such a suggestion borders on madness. And indeed, the setting for the new event, the scenery and all the appearances were as different as the coat and trousers of 1922 were from the flowing robes of the ancient Hebrews. Yet was not the difference only in the shell? Was the essential core so different? Were we not in the presence of a new Moses and a new Aaron who did exactly the same in the context of their time as those venerable figures had done in the wilderness of Sinai? The one a man of God with a unique message who did, however, not assume the priestly office; the other his brother in the spirit who became the first priest of a new dispensation?[19]

Alfred Heidenreich
1898 January 17, Regensburg –
1969 March 11, Johannesburg, South Africa

Alfred Heidenreich was born into a Protestant family – his father was a civil servant – in largely Catholic Bavaria. In the seventh century Regensburg had been Christianised by Celtic monks, and Heidenreich walked past the old 'Schottenkirche' (a name found in a number of cities on the Continent pointing to Iro-Scottish origins) of St Jakob every day on his way to school. He developed a keen interest in history growing up in this ancient city. His classical education consisted largely of Latin and Greek with some French and Italian, as well as mathematics. Heidenreich remembers: 'It was not the sweep of the oratory of a Demosthenes we were led to appreciate, but to realise that a particular form was the third person singular medium plusquamperfekt of one verb or other.'[20]

A keen rambler, like many of his generation, Heidenreich was in the Wandervogel, the youth movement that sought freedom, a sense of adventure and getting 'back to nature. In 1914, when most of the movement's leaders went off to war, Heidenreich became one of the leaders at the age of sixteen.

The idea of following the family tradition of becoming a civil servant (as his older brothers had done) was abhorrent to him. In 1916, having completed his schooling at the top of his class, he was called up to serve in France. Just before the end of the war he was captured and spent a year in British captivity in France, where he learned to read English from a French book on English grammar, but he never had to speak a word of the language. Before his release one of the British guards took him on a clear day and pointed across the Channel to the white cliffs of Dover, saying, 'There, England.' The experience remained with Heidenreich, who felt it like a kind of portent.

On his release in 1919 he studied German and English in Munich. On a student hiking trip he met Marta Heimeran. Each related afterwards how this first meeting was like a deep recognition. Over the following months they got to know each other and for the summer semester they enrolled at Rostock University in the north of Germany. But they spent more time hiking than studying, so they decided to study in separate cities, Heimeran going to Tübingen, Heidenreich back to Munich.

In March 1921 Heimeran persuaded a reluctant Heidenreich to come to a student conference by Rudolf Steiner in Stuttgart on 'Observation of Nature, Mathematics, Scientific Experimentation'. Heidenreich experienced this as a complete eversion, commenting, 'If I stay to the end of this conference, I'll become an anthroposophist.'

During this conference Steiner met with representatives of the youth movement, for which Heidenreich was chosen as spokesman. This led in the following year to Heidenreich's first publication, *Jugendbewegung and Anthroposophie* (Youth Movements and Anthroposophy); the first edition of 5000 copies quickly sold out. Recognising that the values young people were searching for in the Wandervogel youth movement could actually be found in anthroposophy, he wrote, 'Anthroposophy is something for young people, and it is a bitter observation to see how they do not meet each other despite belonging together in their deepest nature.' To try and bridge this divide, together with Wilhelm Kelber he started an anthroposophical youth magazine, *Der Pfad* (the Path).

Alfred Heidenreich in 1968

After the student conference, Heidenreich continued his studies in Tübingen. As well as being together with Marta Heimeran, there were also a number of students actively interested in anthroposophy. Two of them, Tom Kändler and Ludwig Köhler attended a theology course Steiner gave in Stuttgart in June 1921. On hearing their reports of the course, Heidenreich resolved to work for this new religious movement, he attended the Autumn Course in 1921, and from that time on worked purposefully towards its birth.

During the founding, at Rudolf Steiner's suggestion, Heidenreich became the youngest lenker, being ordained as part of the first Act of Consecration of Man on September 16, 1922. He agreed to work in Frankfurt after completing his doctoral studies in Tübingen.

In Frankfurt he started by holding lectures on the Gospel of John.

> I had never read the Gospel of John, I had in fact the utmost difficulties in finding any relationship to it, yet I believed that I must take it as my subject. The first line of the prologue and the raising of Lazarus were the two chinks through which I could get a glimpse of the light enshrined in this unique document.[21]

After his third lecture he asked that people might take turns in giving him one good meal a day. These invitations to lunch 'developed into veritable lunch-hour meetings' that created a congregation, which was founded in June 1923 with a service held weekly from then on. Heidenreich relates that he had 'a peculiar inward problem':

> While from the very start I never felt any difficulty in celebrating the Act of Consecration, I had immense difficulties with the New Testament. In the celebration I felt myself from the beginning with great matter-of-factness as an alchemist who carried out certain sacred processes according to the instructions of the arch-alchemist, the Christ. This I could do with perfect conviction and dedication. But in spite of, or perhaps because of, a Lutheran upbringing I was positively allergic to the New Testament; it took me years to find an access to this, for me, alien territory.
> If this had been simply a personal oddity, I should pass it over in

silence. But I think it was symptomatic. I may, again, have been an extreme case, but not an entire exception. I believe that some of us had to be complete newcomers to the traditional Christian documents, so as to make quite sure that they were rediscovered in complete freshness for the new age. The new springtide of Christianity could do with souls to whom nothing traditional seemed acceptable, if it was to be accepted simply for the sake of being traditional and time-honoured. If this movement was to do its divinely ordained duty, there had to be something 'radically new' in it, to use a phrase which Rudolf Steiner repeatedly used with earnest emphasis.

For the time being, the one and only section from the New Testament which I could read with complete honesty was the fourth chapter of Revelation. And so for weeks my first patient fellow-worshippers had to listen to the same reading every Sunday.[22]

In January 1924 Marta Heimeran was sent to Frankfurt to build the congregation with Heidenreich. In the two years after the founding, Rudolf Steiner held two more courses for priests, the first in Stuttgart in July 1923, the second in Dornach in September 1924 on the Apocalypse. Before the beginning of this course, Heidenreich relates:

In August 1924, in the last but one interview I was able to have with him, Rudolf Steiner himself took the initiative and began to speak about taking The Christian Community to England and America. As far as I am aware, he never brought the subject up on any other occasion...

The interview lasted about 45 minutes. I was allowed to ask a number of questions concerning my personal life. When I had finished, Rudolf Steiner seemed to have still more time. So I ventured to change the subject and asked him whether he saw any prospects of our movement penetrating into Russia. He did not seem to take my question very seriously. He felt that perhaps it had not been asked with a very earnest purpose. He began to tell me stories of Rasputin, as if to indicate what type of man one would have to be in order to make a success in modern Russia. Then he changed his tone, in fact his whole attitude, almost abruptly and became deadly serious. He spoke of Central Europe. 'Germany will have the fate of Greece,' he said. 'If you won't have, within three years, colonies in England and America, you will have nothing more to live on in Central Europe.'

These sentences, for which I can recall every sound and intonation of Rudolf Steiner's voice, were a climax in the last few minutes of the interview. For some reason I buried them deeply in my mind. I believe I never mentioned them to anybody until long after I had settled in England. I certainly did not connect them with anything that I might have to do myself.[23]

In 1928 Friedrich Rittelmeyer was invited to speak at the first anthroposophical World Congress in London, and Alfred Heidenreich spent four weeks in England prior to this conference, staying in Southend-on-Sea (the cheapest place he could find from scanning advertisements). Every morning he would read *The Times* leader to his hostess, thus beginning to train his ear to English sounds. In 1929 he and Marta Heimeran moved to London to set up a new congregation – rather longer than the three years recommended by Steiner.

Heidenreich's grasp not only of the English language, but also of its history, literature and culture was remarkable. In later years one would never have suspected him of being anything other than an Englishman, and on his frequent trips to Germany, he would always take a day or two to 'become German' again. He was not interested in establishing a German congregation in London (though many refugees from the Nazi regime came along), but wanted to root his work in the soil of the country. In this respect he was like St Paul who, when preaching to the Gentiles, did not foist Jewish traditions and the laws out of which Christianity had been born upon them. This was not always accepted by his German colleagues, who sometimes thought he had lost the original impulse.

Heidenreich as lenker (and from 1938 oberlenker) was also responsible for the international movement, and after the banning

1. THE BEGINNINGS OF THE CHRISTIAN COMMUNITY

of the Anthroposophical Society in Germany by the Nazi regime, he was involved in protracted and difficult negotiations to ensure The Christian Community was allowed to continue in Germany. Ellen Huidekoper, who researched this in some detail, wrote:

> There were three delicate points that had to be dealt with: the relation of The Christian Community to anthroposophy, to politics, and also to people of Jewish heritage. The nearness to anthroposophy was the main cause of the present threat of a prohibition. The officials looked at The Christian Community as a daughter movement of the Anthroposophical Society, and since the Society had been forbidden, the daughter also had to disappear ... Rittelmeyer, Lenz and Heidenreich tried to make clear to the officials that the relationship of their church to the Anthroposophical Society was, in reality, much more complex. As an organisation, the church was in no way a daughter, but was a completely independent 'person-in-law' inwardly, however, the priests had a 'natural' connection to anthroposophy. They were not prepared to deny anthroposophy itself or the significance of Rudolf Steiner. Based on this position, some officials advised them to have The Christian Community reallocated to a different classification – from being classed with Freemasonry to coming under the Ministry of Churches. And if The Christian Community would continue to represent itself with strictly religious interests, and without attempts to shelter anthroposophy, then there would be a chance for its survival.
>
> ...'The negotiations would have gone fairly well,' Rittelmeyer, reported to the colleagues, if they would cease to accept Jewish people into the congregations. But they had repeatedly stated that they would not refuse the sacrament to anyone, and that they would stand or fall on this decision. Thus there were certain fundamental principles – among them the equality of all human beings – which The Christian Community stood for as an organisation, and for which it now placed itself at risk of prohibition.[24]

These protracted negotiations (continuing after the outbreak of war when Heidenreich could no longer take part) ensured that The Christian Community could continue working in Germany until it was eventually banned in 1941.

Ever a keen hiker, in the fifties and sixties Heidenreich loved to walk in the Lake District during conferences at Woodford House in Keswick. He was particularly fond of youth conferences, and had a way of answering some of the semi-conscious questions young people carried around with them. His cosmopolitan and practical side could also come to the fore. I remember an occasion when the quarterly production of the youth magazine was getting later and later, and we were trying to plan how to catch up; Heidenreich popped into the room for a few minutes, listened, asked to see the proof copy of the imminent edition, and said, 'It's quite thick, just print "double issue" on the cover, and you'll have caught up.'

Oliver Mathews wrote, 'If this man had gone into politics he would have reached ministerial rank; if a lawyer, he would have been a leading barrister; if he had gone into business he would have become a top executive. Instead, these capabilities have been devoted to religious renewal.'[25] There was always something of the businessman about him when he planned on buying another house to serve the needs of the Community, but sometimes one could glimpse the general who spoke of 'campaigns' and 'headquarters'.

Following Rittelmeyer's death, Heidenreich became an oberlenker together with Gottfried Husemann, first with Bock and then with Frieling. It was not always easy working together. Just before his death, in a conversation with Heinz Maurer, Heidenreich, looking back on his work for the movement, saw the seeds of a deeper harmony in the dissonances he had often experienced, and described himself as 'the pragmatist, Husemann the guardian of the archetypes, and Frieling the mediator.'[26]

In 1969 he flew to South Africa for the induction of Neville Adams in Johannesburg, arriving on Friday morning, March 7. He met colleagues to discuss the practical arrangements. In the evening he gave a talk, 'What is The Christian Community?' – full of warmth and light born out of his experience. Then with

1. THE BEGINNINGS OF THE CHRISTIAN COMMUNITY

*Alfred Heidenreich walking
in the Lake District*

Heinz Maurer, he returned to Cresset House, where he was staying between Johannesburg and Pretoria. In the early hours of Saturday he had a heart attack. He was in pain but could speak clearly. On Saturday there was still the hope that he would be well for Sunday, but two hours before the induction Heinz was with him, and Heidenreich said, 'Heinz, there is nothing for it but to accept the situation. You'll have to induct Neville.'

Just before returning to Cape Town on Tuesday morning, Heinz looked in on Heidenreich, found that he was breathing with great difficulty. Heinz said the Lord's Prayer aloud and Alfred Heidenreich died. It seems characteristic that he did not have a gentle retirement, slowing down and taking it easy, but was fully active and in the midst of things right to the end.[27]

Marta Heimeran
1895 October 2, Nürnberg – 1965 May 2, Arlesheim, Switzerland

Of the three women ordained at the founding of The Christian Community in 1922, Marta Heimeran was the only one who carried her chosen task and mission through to the end of her life. Oliver Mathews wrote of her:

> She must have been in her early thirties when I met her first. She was seventy when she died. During all this time she never gave the impression of being either young or old. Her face expressed something that did not belong to time ... This does not mean that her face never changed. She readily smiled and laughed. She had such genuine joy in so many things, and she could look deeply serious.
>
> Her voice was unusual, a voice that remains in the memory, seldom raised, seldom excited. It was as if something in her voice inwardly – certainly not outwardly – sang and prayed when she spoke.[28]

Kenneth Walsh described her in the 1930s when she was living in London at 1001 Finchley Road:

> She was a person of indomitable courage, strong not to say obstinate will, spiritual purity. She was not an easy person to live with, she did not find herself easy to live with; it was like trying to live with one's better self and often you were aware of your failure, she was aware of hers. Life at '1001' could be difficult – and rations were often short – but there was always a sort of inner luminosity, which emanated from Frau Heimeran and pervaded the house and household.[29]

Her father was a general in the Royal Bavarian Army, and she grew up in a large house with servants in the centre of Nürnberg. At the age of eleven she saw a poster advertising Rudolf Steiner, and insisted on

1. THE BEGINNINGS OF THE CHRISTIAN COMMUNITY

going to his lecture; she understood nothing and was not particularly impressed. She was part of the youth group of Rittelmeyer's church and often heard his sermons.

When she finished school, just before the First World War, she spent some time in Lowestoft in England as an au pair. The war years and her time with the Wandervogel youth movement sparked a wish to work socially, perhaps as a teacher. She was much clearer about what she did *not* want to do – study theology or marry a minister. She studied economics in Munich, and it was there in 1919 that she first met Alfred Heidenreich. They spent the following summer semester at Rostock University in the north of Germany, but did more hiking than studying, and decided to continue their studies in separate cities.

In Tübingen Heimeran met Gerhard Klein and others who were interested in anthroposophy. In March 1921 Steiner held a student conference in Stuttgart. Heidenreich was also invited, but was not interested. Marta Heimeran sent him the programme with the comment, 'Just so you know what you're missing.' He came from Munich.

In autumn 1921 many of her fellow Tübingen students were going to Steiner's theology course in Dornach. Marta Heimeran was ill, and was still unconvinced that there was any future in theology, but she wanted to help this new venture. She arrived there rather late, not yet fully recovered, and Gerhard Klein arranged for her to meet Steiner. She told him of her wish to work socially to bring about a more meaningful culture. To this Steiner replied, 'If you really want to renew culture you must start with religion, with ritual.' From that time on Heimeran was committed to the new religious movement.

She spent the following summer in Ulm looking for people to join the new movement, to start building up a congregation. At the founding in September 1922 she was very busy between lectures sewing the vestments for the new sacraments. Gerhard Klein and Marta Heimeran were servers at the very first Act of Consecration of Man.

Heimeran and Heidenreich planned to marry and Heimeran announced this at the meeting in Breitbrunn. Not only was the idea of women priests completely new, the idea of two priests marrying was unheard of. Heidenreich asked Steiner's opinion on the matter and he received the following simple reply: 'The marriage must be such that it does not affect the dignity of the priesthood.'

After the founding of The Christian Community Heimeran returned to Ulm, working there as a priest until 1924 when she joined Alfred Heidenreich in Frankfurt to found the congregation there. They married in 1929 before moving to London to start work in Britain, partly for the practical reason that it would be impossible for them to rent a room as an unmarried couple.

Their marriage was not easy: she loved him and needed him, but at the same time could not tolerate having him too close. While she started her priestly work immediately after the founding, he went back to university to complete his studies and doctoral thesis. While she worked tirelessly in Frankfurt, Heidenreich as lenker was often travelling, and would return to tell her how things should be done.

In 1932 their son Michael was born – Marta had gone to stay with friends in The Hague for the birth, as conditions in Finchley Road in London were hardly suitable. When she returned with the baby, other members of the Community pushed the baby in a pram around Hampstead Heath during services. (Michael also became a priest in 1962).

Her grasp of the English language was good, but she had difficulties adjusting to the different ways in her new surroundings. She did not find her English colleagues easy to work with, and nor did they with her. Despite her social ideals, her background meant that she was used to giving orders and expected them to be carried out. And English timekeeping was not as precise as in Germany.

In September 1939, just before the outbreak of war, she remained in Germany with her son when Alfred Heidenreich returned to Britain. Unable to join him, she worked in Dresden until the *Verbot* – the closing down of The Christian Community in Germany by the Nazi authorities in 1941. During the *Verbot* she continued celebrating the Act of Consecration in secret, and at these times was always aware of the community of those who had died.

After the war Heimeran and Heidenreich did not resume their life together. She went to Tübingen where she worked for the rest of her life. In 1963 she was made lenker – the first woman since Gertrud Spörri left the movement in 1933.

1. THE BEGINNINGS OF THE CHRISTIAN COMMUNITY

Marta Heimeran

After a visit to Florence for a baptism in 1965 she suffered a stroke and was taken to the anthroposophical clinic in Arlesheim, where she died in the early hours of the same day that four priests (including Julian Sleigh who had been born in Florence) were ordained in London.[30]

First steps

The priests went to their assigned cities, and from Advent 1922 – the beginning of the Christian year – celebrated the Act of Consecration of Man regularly. It was a difficult time financially, as inflation in Germany was heading to hyperinflation. Heidenreich gives us a glimpse of this from his time in Dornach in September 1922:

Even on the purely material level the crossing of the frontier from Switzerland back into Germany was like moving from a prosperous residential suburb into a slum. A small personal experience may illustrate this. While in Dornach I had been put up by kind friends who lived a long way from the Goetheanum. One morning I was late; so my hosts gave me half a Swiss franc to pay for the tram fare. From a German point of view half a franc was a small fortune in those days. I confess that I accepted the gift, but saved it. I made the meeting in time by running a couple of miles. Afterwards that half franc, changed into German inflation marks, paid more than the fare for the express train all the way from Basle to Stuttgart.[31]

There were other difficulties too. In some places the whole local anthroposophical group contemplated changing itself into a congregation of The Christian Community. Heidenreich relates what happened:

We young people were too inexperienced to cope with this situation, and it must also be admitted that some priests were glad to have their services and meetings well attended without much effort on their part.
In this critical situation Rudolf Steiner came to the rescue. And in circumstances of this kind he did not mince his words. He recognised clearly the dangerous tendencies which might turn the Community and the Society into sectarian bodies.
On December 30, 1922, during the last Christmas conference in the first Goetheanum, he devoted a whole evening to this problem of the right relationship between The Christian Community and the Anthroposophical Society. On this occasion he made a very earnest plea that anthroposophists should not simply submerge themselves in The Christian Community. Deeply anxious about the future of the Anthroposophical Society, whose energies, stability, sense of purpose and very economic security might be threatened by the powerful attraction of the new religious movement, he attempted to recall the

1. THE BEGINNINGS OF THE CHRISTIAN COMMUNITY

members of the Anthroposophical Society to their first duty and loyalty by appealing almost to their pride, when he said that anthroposophists should have no need for religious renewal, and that The Christian Community should look after people who cannot take Anthroposophy but simply seek a modern form of the Christian religion. This was a hard saying, and he himself explained a few weeks later (in a lecture given in Stuttgart on January 25, 1923) that it was only his overwhelming anxiety for the safety and wellbeing of the Anthroposophical Society which had wrung these remarks from him. And he continued his explanation by saying: 'How could I possibly wish to criticise in any way whatever this movement for religious renewal? For it came into existence three and a half months ago out of what I myself advised, and it is the most natural thing that the prosperity of this movement should afford me the greatest satisfaction. I think that about this no doubt can exist whatsoever. But I felt compelled already after these three and a half months of [its] activity to speak those words in Dornach ... And these words could not be anything but a paraphrase of this: 'Rejoice in the daughter, but don't forget the mother!'[32]

Nevertheless, the fledgling movement survived and grew, and gradually spread. Rudolf Steiner was able to give the priests two more courses – a brief one in Stuttgart in July 1923, and a longer one about the Apocalypse in September 1924, at the same time as the Pastoral-Medical Course for priests and physicians. Emil Bock describes the last course that Steiner gave:

As priests of The Christian Community we experienced the breath-taking, far-reaching pace from one day to the next in a particularly clear way, not only because we were invited to all courses and evening lectures, but for another special reason: some time earlier Rudolf Steiner had promised us a course on the Apocalypse of St John. At Easter, when he decided to give the Pastoral-Medical Course for doctors and priests, he told us, 'There will still be time for two or three lectures about the

Apocalypse.' Now our course on the Apocalypse started as soon as the Drama Course and the others began. Nothing had been determined beforehand about the length of the courses. After we had received such over-abundance for nearly two weeks day after day, I was given the embarrassing task of asking Rudolf Steiner how long the courses would continue. After all, we did have congregations in those days that expected their regular Sunday service, and we had already once delayed in our return by telegram. Rudolf Steiner answered: 'Please wait a few more days, then it can be determined how long we will continue the courses.' Finally, the Drama Course had grown to nineteen, the Pastoral-Medical Course to eleven, and our course on the Apocalypse to eighteen lectures. It was impossible not to think that this was the farewell, and that Rudolf Steiner still wanted to give as much as was humanly possible.[33]

These were the last lectures Steiner gave. At the end of September 1924 he was so ill that he had stop lecturing. He died on March 30, 1925. Friedrich Rittelmeyer came from Stuttgart to hold his funeral.

Rudolf Frieling
1901 March 23, Leipzig, Germany –
1986 January 7, Stuttgart, Germany

Rudolf Frieling was a quiet, modest man. In his later years his tall frame was bent, but there was still a bright, shining light in his eyes under those big, bushy eyebrows. As erzoberlenker he held ordinations. On such occasions a great number of priests in vestments file into the church before the service begins. After the candidates are led in, the celebrant comes in with the cup. On these occasions you could see Frieling entering as a bent, old man. But then a transformation took place: he stood up straight before the altar and his powerful voice filled the church.

1. THE BEGINNINGS OF THE CHRISTIAN COMMUNITY

Rudolf Frieling in 1938

A brilliant lecturer, painting vivid pictures from history or from the Bible, often he would pick out tiny details from a text and illumine them. His three volumes of biblical studies (*Old Testament Studies, Hidden Treasures in the Psalms* and *New Testament Studies*) are wonderful examples of his attention to detail. His profound knowledge of Greek and Hebrew would also come into play when looking at biblical passages. When teaching at the seminary he would often throw in a little English or French translation for those foreign students who were struggling with the intricacies of the German language.

Frieling was born in Leipzig on March 23, 1901. His father was a Lutheran minister and he grew up with his brothers in idyllic rural surroundings. His sister died when he was three, and the words of the funeral service made such a deep impression on him that he asked his uncle to repeat them to him. The family moved to Chemnitz when Frieling went to school. He experienced both city and school as an oppressive imprisonment of his free spirit, which lived in its own imaginative world. As a child on vacation in Warnemünde on the Baltic coast, he saw the German fleet leaving port. This led to a lifelong (purely mental) connection to the sea, to ships, navies and naval battles.

As a teenager it became clear to him that he wanted to study theology. Aged seventeen he came across Rittelmeyer's article on anthroposophy. He made an independent study of both subjects before starting university and wrote to the famous Rittelmeyer about his doubts in each subject. Showing that quiet, self-deprecating sense of humour that he had throughout his life, his letter began, 'Please excuse me, that as a total stranger I am hijacking your attention by post.'

He studied in Rostock and Marburg where he met Borchart and Johannes Werner Klein, who invited him to the June Course in Stuttgart. When it came to committing to the founding of The Christian Community, Frieling wrote in his memorandum: 'My sheer immaturity (*Grünenjungenhaftigkeit*) weighs down on me. However, I can see that the present situation calls for a beginning to be made soon. I am also clear that the moment will never come when I can say to myself, "Now I am sufficiently mature".'

Together with Johannes Perthel, who had been a Lutheran minister, he founded the Leipzig congregation. Later in life Frieling had an impeccable sense of timing: giving courses at the seminary he would appear just before nine in the morning, get out one or two tiny books from which he might quote, switch on the desk lamp, take a breath, and begin as the church clock struck nine. His lectures (completely without notes) were lively and had many little digressions and anecdotes, but always found their way back to the main thread. Without ever having once looked at his watch he would reach his conclusion, close his books, switch off the lamp, and the church clock would strike ten. However, he found his first lecture in Leipzig an ordeal. He had carefully prepared, pacing the streets of Leipzig the night before to clearly imprint the content on his mind. When it came to the lecture, he got up, said everything he had to say, and sat down. To his horror he found he had spoken for only ten minutes. However, Perthel got up and continued with the subject for another hour as if it had been planned.

1. THE BEGINNINGS OF THE CHRISTIAN COMMUNITY

Rudolf Frieling in 1967

In 1925, during a Christian Community conference in Berlin at which he was giving a number of lectures, he married Margaretha Gayda. In typically modest fashion their honeymoon consisted of an afternoon's bus tour between conference sessions. It was the beginning of a close marriage, without children, that lasted until Margaretha's death in 1969.

While in Leipzig he wrote his doctoral thesis. After completing his thesis he worked briefly in Mannheim and Nürnberg before being sent to Vienna in 1927. There he remained until the *Verbot*. During the *Verbot* he worked for the Viennese Department of Monuments ('The monument that actually needing protecting was myself,' he quipped.) In 1929 he was made lenker of Bavaria, Austria and Bohemia. As lenker he held confirmations, and dutifully learned Czech to be able to celebrate the confirmation service in Prague in the native language.

After the war he worked from Marburg visiting lost and bombed-out congregations in the Ruhr district and in Bavaria. Then in 1949 he and Margaretha went to New York to work with

Verner Hegg in founding a new congregation. He quickly learned English and lectured both for The Christian Community and the Anthroposophical Society. Frieling wrote many articles and books in German, but here in New York he wrote a little gem of a pamphlet that has never been translated into German, *The Metamorphosis of the Eucharist* (since reprinted simply as *The Eucharist*). On his return to Germany in 1954, he passed through Paris and held a lecture in French for the congregation there. No one (who didn't know) suspected Frieling was German – he had such a strong American accent.

In 1954 he returned to Germany, now to Stuttgart where he took up the office of oberlenker until Bock's death in 1960 when he became erzoberlenker.[34]

Rudolf Koehler
1899 December 12, Tetschen, Bohemia –
1992 June 19, East Grinstead, England

Rudolf Koehler's father was a railway employee in Tetschen, Bohemia (now Děčin, Czech Republic) on the Elbe; the main line from Berlin to Prague ran through the town. From the age of ten he attended school in Dresden. In the last two months of the First World War he was called up and served in the artillery in Alsace.

He studied theology in Leipzig (for Old Testament studies he had Professor Rudolf Kittel, editor of *Biblia Hebraica,* the critical edition of Hebrew scriptures, and Alfred Jeremias, expert on the religions of the ancient Near East). He really wanted to be a missionary in China, and started to learn Mandarin, but events took another turn. In Leipzig he heard a lecture by Wilhelm Salewski, which encouraged him to study anthroposophy and take part in anthroposophical meetings in Leipzig. For a time he was an exchange student in Sweden where he learned Swedish. After returning to Leipzig, one day he found a note

1. THE BEGINNINGS OF THE CHRISTIAN COMMUNITY

Rudolf Koehler

on his door: 'I would like to meet you. Rudolf Frieling.' This led to a lifelong friendship, beginning with daily study of anthroposophy.

Koehler was not part of the preparatory meetings of The Christian Community, but he heard Rittelmeyer and Bock speak at a student conference, and then was in Breitbrunn and at the founding. Afterwards he completed his studies in Leipzig where Johannes Perthel and Rudolf Frieling founded the Community.

He was assigned to Bremen in 1923, then to Stuttgart in 1924–25, and at Easter 1925 to St Gallen, where he founded the first Swiss Community. In 1926 he married Bertha Karstensen whom he had met in Bremen, and their first son was born there.

At Advent 1927 he was sent to Vienna with Frieling to re-found the congregation there. (Kurt Willmann had gone there in 1922, but had to stop work for health reasons.) The Koehlers had two more children, a daughter and a son Andreas (1933–90) who also became a priest. During that time he wrote his Ph.D. thesis, 'Because,' he said, 'in Austria without an academic title you are not really a full human being.'

Some priests remain in one place for a long time, others move about often. Koehler seems to have been one of the latter. In 1936 he moved to Leipzig until the Community was banned in 1941. After imprisonment for two months he was called to military service in France and Russia. Immediately after the war he returned to Leipzig to gather the dispersed congregation.

In 1948 when the congregation in New York was founded, Koehler was asked to help in the United States. His earlier wish to work in China was now transformed into the task of working in the West. He spent two years in London learning English and waiting for a work visa. Because of his military service this was not granted, and plans were changed. He took a steamer from Bristol to Montreal in November 1953 and stayed in Toronto, as the Canadian authorities were more welcoming. The Church of The Christian Community in Canada was founded and registered in 1954.

The early days in Toronto were difficult, but now at last Koehler was settled in one place for a greater length of time. He used to visit Quebec and Ottawa regularly, and also Chicago. Ten years later he became lenker of North America, which involved a lot of travelling. After Heidenreich's death in 1969, Koehler went to England to support the work at Shalesbrook, but in 1972 he became an oberlenker and moved back to Stuttgart.

His first wife, who had lived in Stuttgart since the children had grown up, died in 1975. He then married Margaret Roberts (previously engaged to Alfred Heidenreich). After retiring from his position as oberlenker, Koehler returned to England. He outlived his son and both wives (Margaret died in 1991). He died in June 1992, one of the few surviving founders, having worked as a priest for almost seventy years.[35]

Carl Stegmann
1897 March 15, Kiel, Germany –
1996 February 16, Öschelbronn, Germany

Carl Stegmann's parents were working class – his father supervised freight workers and loading in the port of Kiel, and his mother was

1. THE BEGINNINGS OF THE CHRISTIAN COMMUNITY

Carl Stegmann in 1937

a hotel housekeeper. He was the oldest of five children and at the age of fifteen began an apprenticeship as a metalworker. He volunteered for military service at the outbreak of the First World War, serving throughout that period.

In the last years of the war he came across theosophical ideas, and afterwards met Erwin Lang who introduced him to anthroposophy. During this time of high unemployment, Stegmann devoted all his energies to its study, feeling that Steiner understood Marx and the workers better than anyone else. (Though on seeing a lecture advertised, 'The Task of Buddha on Mars' by Rudolf Meyer, he felt there were more pressing problems here on earth.)

While sitting on a park bench Stegmann was accosted by a young man who not only asked for directions, but went on to tell him about anthroposophy and preparations for a new religious movement. Harald Schilling went on to explain that its new service was to be not only for people here but for God, the angels and those who had died. This struck a chord in Stegmann's heart.

Shortly before this he had married Christine in 1921, and with money from her family they were able to attend the East-West Congress in Vienna in 1922, the biggest international public conference with Rudolf Steiner. He made a point of speaking with Friedrich Rittelmeyer.

After the founding he worked in Hamburg with Tom Kändler. We can get a feeling for his work from a comment of Steiner's: 'We could really use such a fiery spirit in our movement.'

In 1927 he moved to Dortmund where he started a workers school and a magazine for social-religious working. Within The Christian Community there was increasing disquiet about his neglecting priestly work. His extensive lecturing activity drew the attention of the Gestapo, but he evaded them by moving to Dornach in Switzerland where he and his wife spent time studying. From 1937 he worked in Mannheim, continuing after the war until 1970.

He became an oberlenker in 1966. Following a visit to the United States in the late 1960s he started his 'America Action', feeling that a concerted effort of The Christian Community in the Bay Area of San Francisco would have far-reaching effects for the future of that continent. In 1970–71 at the age of 73 he moved to Oakland, California with a number of younger priests. Some years later he worked in Sacramento where he helped found what is now Rudolf Steiner College (with a Stegmann Hall).

After fourteen years in America he returned to Mannheim in 1985. When his wife died in 1990 he moved to the old people's home in Öschelbronn where he died on February 16, 1996, aged almost 99 years old. He had worked as a priest for 74 years.[36]

2.
Beginnings in Britain

Within a few years of the founding of The Christian Community in Germany and Austria, congregations were founded in the German part of Switzerland, and in 1926 Heinrich Ogilvie began work in Holland (The Hague then Rotterdam). Just before this in 1925 Eduard Lenz and Josef Král, a newly ordained priest from Bohemia, were sent to Prague, which at this time had a large number of German speakers. In 1927 Christian Smit began working in Norway.

Alfred Heidenreich described these developments and the step into the English-speaking world as follows:

> These countries [Holland, Czechoslovakia, Norway], while having their own language and culture had strong links with German-speaking Central Europe and the majority of educated people could read a German book and follow a German lecture.
> To carry The Christian Community into the English-speaking world was another matter. One would not be able to build on a similar cultural and religious groundwork. One would not be able to use available Christian Community literature in German, which was steadily growing. One would not be able to count on the regular cooperation of German-speaking colleagues and invite them for visits, apart from very exceptional cases. One would have to begin in isolation and from nothing.[1]

In the very first issue of the English *Christian Community Journal*, Leo Baker characterised this essential difference between Central Europe and Britain.

The genius of Middle Europe is, so to speak, vertical. Each man is intensely individualistic, he behaves in a way that expresses the unit rather than the group. He likes a small horizon within which he can discover everything there is to be discovered, by digging deeply and by scaling impossible heights. Like the pines of his great forests, he faces the world and his fellow men with a self-contained vertical glance, and he finds it necessary to remind himself of the possibilities of horizontal contact by constantly shaking hands.

The English genius is horizontal and directly opposed to the German. We like to spread out but not to dig too deeply. We are great colonisers and missionaries. We are members of groups, and discourage the expression of too much individuality. We dress alike, and finish each other's sentences in conversation.[2]

First visits

In 1926 Emil Bock and Walter Krüger (1896–1960) paid two short visits to Britain and then Krüger stayed for six months in 1926–27. Krüger had first experienced the Act of Consecration of Man in 1925 and decided to study for the priesthood, and was ordained in 1927. With Bock's encouragement, he came to Britain as a student, lodging with a family in London to whom he was to teach German conversation for three days in the week. He travelled up and down the country, particularly to the industrial cities of Sheffield and Manchester. From the first he loved England. His innate receptivity and his love of human nature were such that strangers were known to stop him in the street to ask if they might confide in him. In his youthful enthusiasm Krüger soon found three likely English candidates for priesthood, but in the end none of these took it further. (Though one of the three, Arnold Freeman from Sheffield, worked intensively at making anthroposophy more widely known, and founded and edited the annual journal, *The Golden Blade,* later editing it with Adam Bittleston). After ordination Krüger worked in Germany, and had little further contact with Britain.

2. THE BEGINNINGS IN BRITAIN

Walter Krüger

Of the original founding priests only Marta Heimeran and Alfred Heidenreich knew English, and Emil Bock had some grasp of the language. Heidenreich and Heimeran were chosen to make the step of establishing the new movement in Great Britain.

Permanent step to Great Britain

On February 4, 1929 Heidenreich moved to London, which remained his home for the rest of his life. Later in the year he was joined by Marta Heimeran; in September they returned to Germany briefly to get married. They then settled in a one-room attic in Highgate. Their room served as chapel, office, living room and bedroom.

From these tiny beginnings there was intense activity – visiting every conceivable contact address that they had collected, and translating the ritual texts into English together with Cecil Harwood (who later was chairman of the Anthroposophical Society in Great Britain for over thirty years). The final part of this work was done at the bungalow of Robert and Margaret Sargeant in Lancing on the

 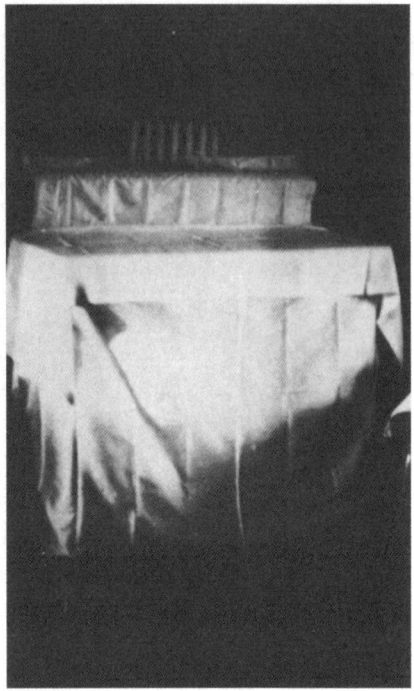

The first room in Highgate, London, that served as chapel, study, sitting room and office

Sussex coast. Mrs Sargeant had known Annie Besant, founder of the Theosophical Society, before her theosophical days, and in 1924 had heard Steiner lecture in London. Here on St John's Day, June 24, 1929, the first Act of Consecration of Man was held in English in the presence of Mr and Mrs Sargeant, Cecil Harwood and Oliver Mathews.³ At the time Heidenreich made the following note in the guest book.

Seven years ago the first group of men and women to start the *Christengemeinschaft* met about this time of the year at a little village by a lake in Bavaria in an old stable. Now we are going to bring our movement to another nation. Again the first group is together in a little village, but the lake has become a sea and the stable a bungalow. May this be a symbol of the growth and strength of our movement to be in this country.⁴

2. THE BEGINNINGS IN BRITAIN

Cecil Harwood (1898–1975), collaborator in the translation of the rituals into English

Croquet on the lawn Lancing; Alfred Heidenreich, Margaret and Robert Sargeant, Marta Heimeran

Within two years Heidenreich and Heimeran's work saw several (modest) English publications, the purchase of a house – the fairy-tale numbered '1001 Finchley Road' – and three English candidates for the priesthood. Leo Baker, Oliver Mathews and Alfred Kaufmann were ordained in August 1931 in Eisenach, Germany, during a Christian Community conference.

In the early 1930s Christian Community services were regularly celebrated in Leeds, Bristol and Wales. Financially things were often difficult; there were times when the priests had to survive with only one meagre meal a day. Hunger, coupled with the tight living conditions, did not always contribute a harmonious working relationship. Nevertheless, the infant congregation grew. Another candidate for priesthood, Adam Bittleston, went to the seminary in Stuttgart and was ordained in 1935. By that time Oliver Mathews was in Leeds, where Adam joined him.

Leo Baker
1898 August 14, London – 1986 September 9, London

Born on August 14, 1898 in London, Leo Baker was an actor with the Old Vic Company in the 1920s. He and his wife operated a handloom-weaving firm in Chipping Campden. They had four children. Baker had wide links in the arts world and was on the fringes of the Inklings, the informal literary group that included Tolkien, C.S. Lewis and Owen Barfield.

After his ordination he worked in Bristol, a city for which Heidenreich had a soft spot as for some reason it reminded him of Weimar. For five years from its beginning in 1932 Baker edited the *Christian Community Journal*. His family lived in London, where his children could go to the New School – the first Waldorf school in Britain, started in Streatham, London in 1925. At the outbreak of war the school was evacuated to Minehead in Somerset (and after the war moved to Forest Row in Sussex where it took the

2. THE BEGINNINGS IN BRITAIN

The first house of The Christian Community in Britain at 1001 Finchley Road, London

Leo Baker, Oliver Mathews, Marta Heimeran, Alfred Heidenreich – the 'British' priests in 1933

name of Michael Hall). When the school was evacuated, Baker and his family moved to Brookthorpe, Gloucestershire so the children could attend Wynstones School, another Waldorf school, and both Leo Baker and his wife took on part-time teaching there. The beginnings in Bristol at 28 Cotham Road and Hillside appear to have been abandoned without much consultation in favour of Gloucestershire. Baker held services regularly at Wynstones School where the school had given The Christian Community a permanent chapel.

The impecunious finances of the Community in those early days made it difficult for a family to survive, and Baker's wife never really supported him in his new vocation. In early 1943 he 'temporarily' accepted a post as Drama Adviser to Gloucestershire County Education Committee.[5] This temporary change became permanent, and Leo Baker never returned to his work with the Community, and broke off all contact.

Michael Tapp visited him in 1982 near Guildford. Baker was still in the world of theatre, and had founded his own theatre school. He had kept up his contact with Owen Barfield through all the intervening years (Barfield died in 1997 at the age of 99). Tapp reported that there seemed to be a lingering bitterness about the financial hardships the family had to endure.

However, we should not underestimate the courage it took to enter into this new and 'foreign' religious movement. And Baker's many contributions in the early journal show fresh and brilliant insights and a sureness of language. Leo Baker died on September 5, 1986.[6]

Alfred Kaufmann
1902 December 22, Stanmore, Sydney – 1986 March 16, Sydney

Kaufmann probably came across anthroposophy through the Rudolf Steiner Bookshop while staying in London in the late 1920s. While

2. THE BEGINNINGS IN BRITAIN

Alfred Kaufmann

warden of the YMCA hostel there he met Stanley Drake whom he introduced to The Christian Community.

After ordination he visited Leeds regularly with Marta Heimeran, holding lectures there every three weeks. However, Kaufmann soon found that the priesthood was not for him, and left after eighteen months.

Kaufmann returned to Australia where he worked for the Australian International Affairs Organisation. Michael Tapp visited him at his home in the centre of Sydney where he had collected numerous artefacts from his extensive travels. Kaufmann kept up a loose contact with The Christian Community, often attending services when he travelled in North America or Europe, but quietly sitting in the back, without ever revealing who he was.

Kaufmann died in Sydney on March 16, 1986. It seems strange that Kaufmann and Baker, two of the first three native English-speaking priests, who both then left the movement, should die a few months apart.[7]

Oliver Mathews
1900 April 5, Birmingham – 1988 January 31, Stourbridge

Oliver Lewis Mathews was born on April 5, 1900 in Birmingham. The family was nonconformist, and his father was a surveyor and land agent. Lonely at boarding school, he was a keen Boy Scout with a love of nature and of walking. He was undergoing army training when the First World War came to an end. As the eldest son, he joined the family business with a view to becoming a partner in it, but came to feel that this was not his calling. Through Captain Field, a teacher at what became Michael Hall School, Oliver met anthroposophy, and attended the first anthroposophical World Congress in London in 1928, where he spoke with Friedrich Rittelmeyer (through an interpreter) without knowing who he was.

He studied theology at Manchester College, Oxford, a Unitarian college. Early in 1929, he was asked to look after a German visitor, Alfred Heidenreich, and soon knew without a doubt that what Heidenreich was seeking to establish was his calling. He was present at the first English Act of Consecration of Man. Two years later Oliver Mathews was one of the first three English-speaking priests ordained in The Christian Community.

He began work in London as chaplain to a Unitarian mission with an agreement that he could work with The Christian Community at the same time. This situation lasted for three years. Then in 1934 he moved to Leeds where he ran a large guest house as a Christian Community centre. There he met Inga Scheck who became his wife in 1938. Inga had fled Germany after the Nazis found out that she had helped Jewish friends. She continued to help many Jewish friends and members of The Christian Community flee Germany by providing them with an address in Britain. Over the next ten years Oliver and Inga had four children.

When the Second World War broke Oliver moved back to London, from where he visited various parts of the country to hold services. Oliver visited his home city of Birmingham regularly and

2. THE BEGINNINGS IN BRITAIN

Oliver Mathews in 1952 in Wales

The hut in the garden that served as chapel in Stourbridge

lived there after the war. In 1947 he moved to Stourbridge, where Elmfield Rudolf Steiner School had opened in 1946, and he worked there for the rest of his life. In 1956 a modest hut was erected in the garden to serve as a chapel. Thirty years later he gave his blessing to the decision to build a chapel on that site. The new, permanent chapel was consecrated in September 1988, a few months after Oliver died.

In 1962 Oliver became lenker of Great Britain. Alfred Heidenreich still lived in London and as oberlenker went regularly to meetings in Germany. However, it was not easy for Oliver, as in effect Heidenreich remained in control. When Heidenreich died in 1969, Oliver was almost seventy, by which time he no longer had the energy to oversee the growing number of congregations. In 1974 Michael Tapp became lenker.

Oliver was quintessentially English, but not the cosmopolitan citizen of the world that Heidenreich was. He remained firmly rooted in Middle England, spending almost his entire life in the Midlands. However, this did not mean he was cut off from the world; he had an enduring interest in social issues. He celebrated the Act of Consecration in Gloucester prison for many years. (He was invited by the prison authorities because one of their inmates, who had only heard the name, claimed that he was a member The Christian Community and wanted to take part in its services.) The Mathews' house was always open for those who needed help or advice, and the Mathews helped some prisoners on their release. He was also known to give shelter to tramps in the garden shed. It cannot be said that his congregation grew as a result of this, but he was known and respected in the town for his practical, Christian attitude.

Oliver was also interested in keeping an open dialogue with other denominations, and was on occasion asked to give sermons in Baptist or Anglican churches. He wrote numerous articles over the years, and in 1981 a collection of his biblical commentaries was published, *The Bible: Unclaimed Legacy*. He also had a great sense of humour, which showed itself in his storytelling, his impersonations using just facial expressions, and in his writing too. There is an article in a youth magazine of the 1950s entitled 'Cricket, the Religion of the

Englishman', in which he wrote of the significance of the three stumps of the wicket as an image of the Trinity, the eleven players in each team the disciples (without Judas?).

Oliver's health declined, and in 1984 he and Inga moved to a retirement home. He died on January 31, 1988, just before his 88th birthday.

Oliver's conviction of the rightness of his path never wavered throughout his life, sometimes leaving him isolated or lonely. Michael Tapp wrote about his integrity and openness:

> He had an abiding trust that in difficult situations others could be as open as he was. Here too he was an optimist. Unfortunately reality was often different. Perhaps to such an honest soul as Mathews' the world appears simpler than it is in reality. But on the other hand, one could rightly say that if all people could be open and honest, the world would actually be different, and perhaps simpler ... I suspect his integrity had far greater effects than we noticed.[8]

Adam Bittleston
1911 December 11, Ockley, Surrey – 1989 May 25, Forest Row, Sussex

Adam Bittleston was a very unusual person. He was tall and one had the impression that his legs hung from his body rather than supporting it. His school friend Alistair Macdonald described him as a schoolboy: he 'looked very much as he did in later life ... He surveyed the world in a benevolent "professorial" way; his face seemed to consist of a number of "Os" – round eyes, round glasses and a mouth that tended to become round and mobile when he was trying to find the appropriate words for something.'[10]

He was brilliant and wise, and loved ideas that were opposite or paradoxical, often being able to reconcile them. He gave many lectures, and no matter how remote the subject, he always included a quotation from Shakespeare. Not only was he an inspiring speaker, but he was a deep listener, as Michael Jones wrote: 'The power to listen was a practical metamorphosis of his far-reaching widths of soul, and was so accepting that you could find yourself saying perhaps more than you intended and even more than you knew about yourself.'[11]

But for all his clarity and order in thinking, when it came to practical matters, Adam somehow never quite belonged to this world. He had a weak constitution, and was lacking in awareness of his dress and general appearance, as well as of his surroundings. Unmatching socks, a mislaid wallet, several unfinished cups of coffee, or a borrowed book might be found under a pile of newspapers or in the bathroom. Peter Button, a colleague with a wry sense of humour, was once visiting, and the next morning told Adam of 'a strange experience' he had had on going to bed. He had browsed through the bookshelves for something to read, found a familiar book, and on opening it 'saw my name written inside'. Without embarrassment or apology, Adam replied, 'Yes, a great number of visitors have that experience.'

He had his share of human failings and frailties. He had several extramarital affairs and at least two illegitimate children, and as a colleague he was not always easy to work with.

Adam Bittleston's parents had married in South Africa where his older sister Kalmia was born. Adam was born in 1911 in Ockley, Surrey, and spent his early childhood near Dartmoor and later in Wiltshire. When he was confirmed in the Church of England he recalls, 'my first communion brought the clear recognition that we are surrounded by another world ... I felt that I was within a great cloud of light which was at the same time boundless goodness and helpfulness.'

Kalmia and Adam were always close, and as children they read and told each other stories, often of other worlds. After prep school, which he felt was 'a Department of Hell', he went to King's School, Burton, where under the liberal spirit of the headmaster he seemed to survive. There he made lasting friendships with several boys who became interested in Rudolf Steiner's work, like David Clement, later

2. THE BEGINNINGS IN BRITAIN

*Adam Bittleston in his
early thirties [Stella East]*

chairman of the Biodynamic Farming Association. Adam was soon reading not only published books but also duplicated lecture cycles from the Anthroposophical Library in London.

Adam was awarded a scholarship at Brasenose, Oxford, where again he found a group of students wanting to study anthroposophy. The group invited various speakers like Cecil Harwood, Captain Field, Alfred Heidenreich, and many others, who often spoke at great length. His friend and fellow student Kenneth Walsh relates:

> On one occasion, however, when Adam himself was speaking, the talk could not go on too long. We all sat spellbound.
> The meeting took place in a medieval room with a capacious chimneybreast. Adam stood with his back to the fireplace and his fingers up the chimney. Every now and again, with a characteristic gesture, he would wipe his brow and gradually, before our very eyes, turned himself into a blackamoor. We watched with bated breath and at the end burst into an unaccustomed round of applause.[12]

Adam and Kalmia visited Dornach in 1929 and met Ita Wegman, leading to Kalmia's working with Wegman for some years. Around 1932, while in his final year at Oxford, Adam Bittleston formed the intention of training for the priesthood, and in 1934 went to the seminary in Stuttgart where he was ordained in 1935. He began work in Leeds with Oliver Mathews. The tiny Community there could not really support two priests, and Adam soon began giving evening classes at the Workers Educational Association (which grew to five evenings a week). In 1937 he married Gisela Hermann, whom he had met in 1933. Daniel and Stella were born soon afterwards.

In a move intended to consolidate the small force of priests in Britain, in 1942 Adam moved to London, where for the first time he experienced a real congregation. Then in 1946, following an invitation to send a priest on a visit to America, Adam spent some months there, giving lectures, holding services, christening many children, holding marriages and even a funeral service.

In 1950 he moved to Edinburgh where he worked for 21 years, first alone and later with Taco Bay. His love and knowledge of Shakespeare was equal to that of an academic specialist, and he always sought to show the relevance of the Bard's characters to the present day. As well as lecturing widely, he wrote many articles and books. These were usually dictated, the finished polished sentences having been formed in his mind, and only rarely did he change the phrasing when he saw the typed version. Taco Bay told how he would sometimes have a few half-formed ideas for a contemplation in the monthly printed programme of the congregation's activities in Edinburgh, which Adam could transform into a cohesive little article within half an hour.

In 1967 a training course for the priesthood in English was established at Shalesbrook, Forest Row, in close cooperation with Emerson College. Soon after Heidenreich's death in 1969 Adam moved to Sussex to take over the leadership of Shalesbrook, and also taught at Emerson College. This began what were perhaps the happiest and most fruitful years of his life. He wrote several books, renewed his friendship with William Golding (whom he first met when they were students at Oxford) and as well as teaching many students, had

2. THE BEGINNINGS IN BRITAIN

Adam Bittleston

*The Heidenreich family in
Finchley Road with Adam Bittleston*

countless meetings with people seeking guidance and advice about their life.

On a trip to America in 1976 he had a fall from which he never fully recovered. He needed a hip replacement operation, which was unsuccessful, leaving him crippled and in pain for the rest of his life. No longer able to celebrate services, he continued to teach, and even when bedridden, had many students come to visit him.[13]

Growth in London

In London the Community house in Finchley Road, with its tiny chapel, was too small for regular services, and a studio at Chalk Farm was rented in 1938. Three members of the original Community in London went on to study at the seminary in Stuttgart – Stanley Drake, Evelyn Francis and Kenneth Walsh.

Walsh 'found it impossible at the time to take any decision which might compromise my freedom of action in the future.'[14] He was not ordained, and instead became a civil servant. After the war, as part of the Allied Control Commission in postwar Germany, he developed the idea of twinning German and British towns as a way of building social, cultural and commercial bridges between the two countries. He was also instrumental in helping The Christian Community start again in Germany. He remained close to the Community and for many years was on its board of trustees.

In June 1939 an ordination service was held – for the first time in England – for Stanley Drake and Evelyn Francis. Emil Bock came from Germany to London to hold the service in German, with Heidenreich repeating each part in English.

Afterwards, as was usual every summer, Heidenreich and Heimeran went to the Continent for meetings and conferences as the storm clouds of war gathered over Europe. Evelyn Francis also visited Germany and Holland that summer.

2. THE BEGINNINGS IN BRITAIN

Stanley Drake

Stanley Drake
1906 August 9, London – 1986 April 5, Watford

Stanley Drake was born in Winchmore Hill, Enfield, north of London. His father was a clerk with the London waterworks. His mother died before he was two years old. After attending boarding school at Tonbridge, where his music master instilled a lifelong love of music in him, he followed his father, becoming a bookkeeper at the waterworks.

In 1934 Stanley was living at the YMCA in London, where he met Alfred Kaufmann who by then was working there. Through Kaufmann (who no longer worked as a priest) he came into contact with The Christian Community. He seems to have found an immediate home there, for by the end of 1935 he was at the seminary in Stuttgart. His ordination was a few weeks before the outbreak of war. He worked in London during the war and for some years afterwards.

In the early days space was so cramped in 1001 Finchley Road that Stanley slept under the desk in the office and every morning pulled a curtain around the desk to hide his 'bedroom'. In 1941 he married Elsie Wright, and their daughter Rosemary was born in 1944.

After the war the London Waldorf school, which had been evacuated during that time to Somerset, settled in Forest Row, Sussex, some 30 miles (50 km) south of London. Stanley made contact with people there who were interested in taking part in the Community, moving there in 1952 with his family. He worked there for the rest of his life. Elsie died in 1964 and Stanley married Margaret Gregg in 1966.

Superficially the first thing one noticed with Stanley was his stammer, which came to the fore particularly when celebrating. It was not really a stutter, but a struggle beginning at his feet and moving up until the words began to flow out, then apparently effortlessly. However, his actions were so clear and the words said so beautifully that it largely went unnoticed. Stanley was very musical and enjoyed singing: he never had any trouble with his words when singing.

He died suddenly on April 4, 1986. He had been too ill to celebrate services for some time, but a week earlier, on Good Friday, had sung in the choir at the chapel with a brief solo. Thus he bade farewell to his congregation in singing. On his way to his granddaughter's confirmation in Stourbridge he took ill, was taken to hospital in Watford where he seemed comfortable, but then died later that night.

His lasting legacy is *Though you Die*, a thought-provoking book that was much in demand, going through a number of editions. When he wrote it in the early 1960s death was a subject that was rarely spoken of. He also wrote a book about birth, and many articles on translations of the New Testament.[15]

2. THE BEGINNINGS IN BRITAIN

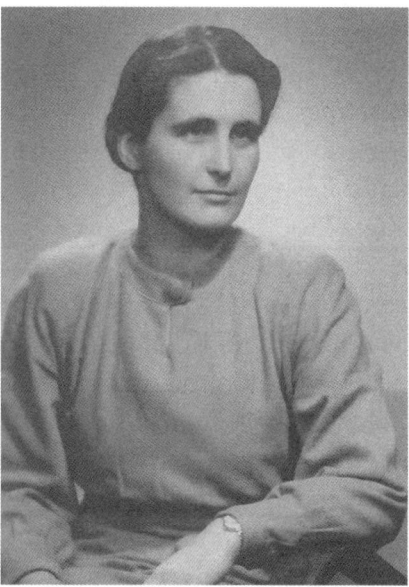

Evelyn Francis

Evelyn Francis
1911 March 23, Stow-on-the Wold, Glos. –
2000 January 5, Tonbridge, Kent

Evelyn was one of five sisters, and came from a Nonconformist religious background. At school she was brilliant, scoring the highest marks in the whole of England in her school certificate. She read modern history at Somerville College, Oxford, and became a management trainee with the catering firm J. Lyons and Co., where a lucrative future beckoned.

She came across Steiner's ideas, became acquainted with The Christian Community through Kenneth Walsh, and became part of the congregation at '1001'. One of her jobs there was to take out the Heidenreichs' baby, Michael, in a pram while the service was held. (Years later after Evelyn had retired and could no longer walk, Michael visited her in Tonbridge, and pushed her out in her wheelchair, while she reminded him of those days.)

85

After her ordination she worked in London, and travelled up and down the country visiting the Community's scattered congregations. Towards the end of the war she found a house in Glenilla Road that was purchased to become a social centre for the Community, and Evelyn lived there. Immediately after the war she managed to travel to the synod and ordination in Holland in December 1945. As Heidenreich still had a German passport he was unable to travel abroad, so Evelyn in effect became the emissary from Britain. Probably through Kenneth Walsh, for a year or so she joined the Allied Control Commission in postwar Germany with the rank of colonel and had responsibility for religious affairs. She helped rebuild Christian groups and churches of all denominations, including The Christian Community.

In 1951 Evelyn married Samuel Derry, the manager of Rudolf Steiner House. Around this time she was asked to work in Bristol. However, the thought of leaving London caused her profound shock and a breakdown. This led to a rift in the London congregation between the north, now based in Glenilla Road, and Evelyn's group, who looked for another centre in west London.

Initially services were held in a flat in Grosvenor Square, but in 1954 Colonel and Mrs Innes (she was in the congregation) offered Evelyn the lower part of their house in 34 Draycott Place, Chelsea. The place was named Benen House after the first of the Irish saints to follow St Patrick. Benen House was never going to be a permanent home, and in 1959 a Georgian house in Hammersmith was found – Temple Lodge at 51 Queen Caroline Street. It had once been the home of the artist Frank Brangwyn (1867–1956), and his studio later became the chapel and then a restaurant. Despite the owner being a builder, the property was in poor condition, and wartime bomb damage made some parts of the building inaccessible. However it went on to become a unique place among Christian Community centres, as it provided accommodation (extended and improved over the years), had a bookshop and later a vegetarian restaurant.

Sadly Samuel Derry died in 1960 just before Evelyn moved into Temple Lodge. A friend suggested she should get away on a holiday and visit South Africa. She took her friend's advice and went to South

2. THE BEGINNINGS IN BRITAIN

Evelyn Francis in later years

Africa for a few months, but she didn't have a holiday. Her days were filled with consultations and services, with visiting people and holding lectures. This was an important step to establishing The Christian Community in South Africa.

In 1967, back in London once more, she married Herbert Capel, who was an indefatigable worker in improving the house, and from the 1980s also printing Evelyn's books – the beginning of Temple Lodge Publishing. Bert Capel died suddenly in 1986. (At different times of her life Evelyn was known as Francis, Derry and Capel. In this book, for simplicity and to avoid confusion, I have generally called her Evelyn Francis.)

Evelyn was a prolific writer. Sevak Gulbekian, who has run Temple Lodge Publishing since 1988, remembers:

> On settling on a theme for a new book – often in response to a specific request – Evelyn would visit her long-term friend Miss Parton (whom she always addressed formally out of respect) and dictate many pages in a single sitting. After a few weeks she would return triumphantly to the office clutching a new

manuscript. But once the book was written, she generally had little further interest in it – instead looking forward to the next project.[16]

Above all, Evelyn was a pastor and counsellor. She was always ready to help people in crisis, and always responded to requests to visit. She travelled to Portugal in 1989 for a christening, and while there celebrated the first Act of Consecration of Man in Portugal (on May 8).[17] In 1993 and 1994 she made trips to Ghana where she had been invited to hold a marriage service. And in 1995 she gave a course on spiritual counselling in São Paolo, Brazil.

In 1997 Evelyn retired aged 86 and, now infirm, was cared for in Tonbridge Wells, where she died on January 5, 2000.

In her active years Evelyn was a true pioneer in every sense. She was willing to learn from new situations and to find a way to penetrate them with her ideals and endeavours. She could at times be headstrong and wilful, and she was not always easy to work with. But her brilliance shone when she lectured, always lively and sprinkled with humour and anecdotes. Having described a shining comet, Peter Allan said of her, 'Whenever Evelyn was at her best, her light-filled words enlivened the chosen theme in a similar way.'[18]

3.
Wartime and Postwar Years

In August 1939 Heidenreich and Heimeran were on holiday in Austria. Heidenreich was to attend the international conference of The Christian Community in Holland at the beginning of September. Marta Heimeran decided to remain in Austria to finish her book about religion and young children.

Following the invasion of Poland on September 1, 1939, Britain issued an ultimatum to Germany to withdraw by 11 am on September 3. On September 2 friends urged Heidenreich to leave, took him to Rotterdam and found a place on a ship to Britain. He arrived next morning at immigration in Britain just before the clock struck 11. The immigration officer looked at his German passport, and without a word let him pass. A minute later he would have been arrested as an 'enemy alien'. As he arrived at the station in London, Neville Chamberlain's declaration of war was being broadcast over the station loudspeakers. When he arrived at '1001' he found Oliver Mathews and Stanley Drake in residence, as they had no longer reckoned on his returning.

In December 1939 he had to appear before a tribunal that classed him as a 'friendly alien'. The critical time came between May and July 1940 when all Germans and Austrians – regardless of whether they were refugees from the Nazi regime or not – were interned, mainly on the Isle of Man (as, for instance, all the founders of Camphill were). By some miracle this did not happen to Heidenreich. In a letter to Heimeran after the war, he describes that a Labour MP intervened with the Home Office.[1] It is also possible that Adam Bittleston asked his uncle, Lord Halifax, to put in a good word with the authorities.

For a time, he had to get a permit to travel outside London, but this was never refused. (After the war Heidenreich was offered British citizenship, a rare honour, as most people wishing to become British had to go through a lengthy procedure of applying for it.)

Marta Heimeran remained in Germany, and they never resumed their marriage, though they were in close contact until her death in 1965.

Evelyn Francis, who was also at the international conference in Holland returned to Britain two days after war had been declared. At a synod held in early September, the priests decided immediately to intensify the celebration of the Act of Consecration of Man – it was held daily in London. After the initial phoney war became real, every Saturday the service included a sermon for those who had died, which began and ended with Steiner's meditative verse for the war dead ('Spirits ever watchful ...').

First years of the war

In London and other cities, schools were immediately evacuated to the countryside, and many families left London, including members and friends of the Community. Several of the early groups and congregations who were visited by priests were a result of the exodus from London. (Leo Baker's family left London for Gloucester, where his children went to Wynstones School.) There were seven priests in Britain at this time: Heidenreich, Francis, Drake and Mathews in London, Baker in Gloucester, and in Leeds Bittleston was joined by Käthe Wolf-Gumpold, a priest of Jewish origin, who had escaped from Germany to Britain just before the war.

With blackouts and restricted transport after dark there were no more evening events. However, a summer conference was held in 1940 near Gerrards Cross, Buckinghamshire (at the time of the invasion threat and first extensive air raids). In London, the studio in Chalk Farm with its glass roof was largely untouched by air raids (only in spring 1945 did a V-bomb hit the roof, and it had to be covered in corrugated iron). Sometimes sirens would go off during the Act of Consecration of Man, but no one left.

3. WARTIME AND POSTWAR YEARS

In 1942 Adam Bittleston moved from Leeds to London, and Käthe Wolf-Gumpold, was finally released from internment on the Isle of Man. Now all the priests were in London, which consolidated their forces; as well as holding services in Hampstead, Golders Green and Streatham in London, they made regular visits to Gerrards Cross, Capel (Surrey) and Brighton, and further afield to Leeds, Sheffield, Wynstones (Gloucester), Birmingham and Clent (near Stourbridge). There were occasional services in Aberdeen and Port Eynon (Swansea, Wales).

Käthe Wolf-Gumpold
1888 May 16, Erfurt, Thuringia –
1961 May 11, Musselburgh, Scotland

Born in 1888, Käthe Wolf-Gumpold had been ordained as a Christian Community priest in 1924. She had been to art and craft college, got married, had two children, and separated. As a priest she worked mainly in and around Stuttgart. After 1935 under Nazi

Käthe Wolf-Gumpold

regulations she was unable to work as a priest in Germany as she was Jewish. She trained in eurythmy, speech and painting, and in late 1938 she managed to come to Britain (though her English was rather limited), initially working in Leeds. For some inexplicable reason the authorities imprisoned her as an 'enemy alien' in Holloway Prison at the beginning of the war; later she was interred on the Isle of Man. At least there, among the many German and Austrian refugee-internees, she could celebrate the service daily, hold study groups, reading circles, put on the Oberufer Christmas plays, and even hold a christening.

She was only released in May 1942 after much lobbying of the Home Office. She was invited to stay for a few weeks with a Community member near London; this turned into three years. After the war she became part of the work in London, but her eyesight deteriorated to the extent that she found walking in London's traffic dangerous. She retired in 1954, living in a large country house near Edinburgh belonging to John Fletcher, a wealthy member. Despite her poor eyesight she studied William Blake's writings and paintings, writing the first major German book on Blake (it was later translated and published in English). She died in May 1961 after a long illness.[2]

The Christian Community on the Continent

In Germany The Christian Community was allowed to continue despite several local attempts to stop its activities. However, when Rudolf Hess fled to Scotland in May 1941, there was a major clampdown on many organisations in Germany. This time The Christian Community was included. On June 9, 1941 The Christian Community was banned in Germany and Austria. Priests arriving at the synod in Nürnberg were arrested and imprisoned, their homes searched and their books confiscated. Most of the priests were released a short time later, some were called up, and the rest went into civilian jobs. Emil Bock was in a concentration camp for eight months before being released.

3. WARTIME AND POSTWAR YEARS

On May 8, 1942 The Christian Community was banned in Bohemia. Josef Adamec, the only priest in Prague at that time, was also arrested. On May 27, 1942, as he was about to be released, the telephone rang. The officer was visibly shocked, and hastily ushered Adamec out. It was only afterwards Adamec discovered that the phone call was informing the officer about an assassination attempt on Reinhard Heydrich. Heydrich was a high-ranking SS officer and Acting Reich-Protector of Bohemia and Moravia; some historians have described him as the darkest figure within the Nazi elite. Heydrich died of his wounds some days after the assassination attempt. There were severe reprisals and many arrests, and had Adamec been summoned for release any later he would not have been freed.

In occupied Holland (with half a dozen priests) and Norway (where Christian Smit worked alone) The Christian Community was able to continue but with restrictions. And in neutral Switzerland (some three priests) and Sweden (where Karl Engqvist worked alone) it continued unhindered. In these countries and in England, the priests were very conscious of their work keeping the flickering flame of The Christian Community alight for the future.

Middle and end of the war in Britain

Soon everything was rationed, including paper, so the printed journal ceased at the end of 1940. It was replaced by a duplicated newsletter that went out unfailingly every month until 1946, largely thanks to Stanley Drake's tireless efforts of gathering material, typing, duplicating and sending it out. Until 1941 the German journal arrived through friends in the (then still) neutral United States, and occasionally articles translated from this appeared in the newsletter. It also included snippets of news about the Community in Germany that sporadically arrived through Switzerland or Sweden (through German and British military censors). During 1942 subscribers increased from just under two hundred to almost three hundred. And in 1943 Adam Bittleston's *Meditative Prayers* was first issued as a duplicated booklet.

In the newsletter in 1942 there was an appeal for wine for the Act of Consecration of Man. The stock of biodynamic unfermented grape juice obtained from Germany before the war had run out. The only grape juice available in Britain had added sugar and the only red wines had distilled alcohol added. Incense, too, had to be made.

During 1941 and 1942 Heidenreich developed a sore in his eye and then a kidney stone. He described this as if the ban on the Community in Germany was affecting his health, despite only hearing of the ban later through a letter from Switzerland.[3] He was sent on several extended recuperation leaves to friends near Aberdeen. While there he visited the new Camphill School for children with learning disabilities and met Karl König; from this initial meeting the links with the Camphill movement were forged. Later extended visits to the north also led to beginnings of the congregation in Aberdeen, which Eileen Hersey then took on in 1944.

Together with the Anglican Venerable A.P. Shepherd (later Canon of Worcester), Reverend George MacLeod of the Church of Scotland (founder of the Iona Community) and a Congregational minister, Heidenreich started a Ministers' Fellowship for the Study of Rudolf Steiner. This group met for several days twice a year. Heidenreich had always sought contact with other denominations, attending the World Conference on Faith and Order in Edinburgh in 1937. Later Will Sawkins and Donald Perkins found their way to The Christian Community through this group.

Early in 1943 Leo Baker dropped out of the work, but late 1943 and 1944 also saw considerable development. The Christian Community was granted charitable status (doubling the value of gifts from taxpayers at the rate of tax in force at that time), and it was recognised as a church, which made its ministers exempt from national service. Houses were purchased for the Bittleston and Drake families. That same year a house in Leeds (with four acres of garden), one in Aberdeen, and the following year one in Birmingham, were acquired.

In London, the studio in Chalk Farm where services were held was sufficient for regular services and meetings, but was unsuitable for any kind of social gathering, and '1001' was simply too small. Despite the dearth of houses in London, through a truly extraordinary sequence of circumstances after Evelyn Francis followed up on a hint, the house in Glenilla Road, Hampstead, was bought at Christmas 1943. It was fifteen minutes' walk from the studio, had rooms that could be let and space for a library, as well as a large room and hallway for Community events. It even had an adjoining site with permission for building. Evelyn Francis ran Glenilla Road as a social centre.

By this time there were three more candidates for ordination. Normally decisions on ordination were taken by the oberlenkers together with some lenkers. However, contact with senior colleagues in Germany was cut off, and Heidenreich kept delaying decisions, hoping for an end of the war so he could communicate with Bock and others. But the war dragged on, and after consulting with the entire priest circle in Britain, he ordained Kalmia Bittleston, Eileen Hersey and Peter Roth in October 1944. It was the first time the ordination service had been held only in English. Kalmia Bittleston was sent to Leeds, Eileen Hersey to Aberdeen, and Peter Roth was to work in London, freeing Oliver Mathews to go to Birmingham.

Eileen Hersey
1901 April 7, London – 1986 May 4, London

Born in London on Easter Sunday, April 7, 1901, Eileen Hersey grew up in comfortable circumstances, enjoyed a private education and then took a degree in history, followed by a diploma in education at Cambridge. In her twenties she was active in Quaker-inspired peace and social work, as well as for the Howard League for Penal Reform.

In 1924 for three months she visited a Quaker family in Frankfurt, staying in the house in which Marta Heimeran and Alfred Heidenreich celebrated services, but she never met them. She was involved in editing the journal of the International Fellowship for Reconciliation,

Eileen Hersey and Alfred Heidenreich

and in 1928 attended its youth camp in Holland where she briefly met Hilmar von Hinüber, a German Christian Community priest with strong social ideals, but nothing came of it. In 1929 she went to Palestine to teach in an Arab Christian girl's school.

She returned to Britain after becoming seriously ill in 1935, and through a fellow Quaker, Alice Nike, she heard of anthroposophy. Some years later she decided to work for The Christian Community and initially became secretary at '1001'. She was completely dedicated to Heidenreich, and he in turn found her to be a good listener who had discretion. She brought her historical and literary talents in helping Heidenreich edit the *Christian Community Journal*. This continued after her ordination in October 1944, and after Heidenreich's death in 1969 she took on editorship of the journal and of the Christian Community Press.

Heidenreich's lengthy visits to Camphill and Aberdeen in the 1940s had resulted in a group of people interested in the work in Scotland. Eileen was sent there after ordination and started the congregation in the newly acquired house in Carden Place. After two or three years she went to Albrighton Hall in Shropshire until it closed in 1953. From that time on she worked in London again until her retirement in 1981.

In 1968, at an age when most people would retire, with Heidenreich's encouragement Eileen paid a first visit to Australia and New Zealand to visit subscribers of the journal, and to see whether it would be possible to found The Christian Community there. She made two more visits in 1971 and 1974, paving the way for the founding in 1988.

Even in old age and despite her busy life, there was always something youthful in Hersey. She never lost her concerns for the world and her interest in people. Michael Tapp describes this:

> On her last visit to Germany for a synod I remember vividly coming across her on a park bench having made warm friends with an elderly German lady who had already told her life story. It was all done with an apparent naivety which simply unlocked the hearts of those 'accosted'. Many are the people who felt her as a friend and companion, and this is perhaps what characterised her work as a priest most. She did not impose herself in any way, which is not to say that there were not times when she knew what she wanted and was quite determined in pursuing it. But it was done with grace, as befitted one born in 1901.[4]

The domestic scene was not her strength:

> Her Faustian bed-sitting room, part study, part chapel, part tea-room, part monastic cell was stuffed with learned and spiritual mementos, mostly books but interspersed with items acquired on long blessed travels of long ago, sometimes propped up by equally long-forgotten biscuits in odd tins anxiously provided by some troubled and concerned visitor.[5]

After retirement in 1981 her health declined, and she died on May 4, 1986.[6]

Kalmia Bittleston
1909 June 10, Pietermarizburg, South Africa –
1989 June 3, London

Kalmia's father was an army officer who was posted to Natal in 1907. There he married Kathleen Dundas who was related to the aristocratic Dundas and Halifax families. Kalmia was born in South Africa, but moved to Surrey in England soon afterwards. Her brother Adam was born there. She only had a few years of formal schooling, the rest she was taught by her mother. She trained to teach in a Montessori kindergarten and during this time a friend introduced her to anthroposophy. She (and Adam) both became members of the Anthroposophical Society before they were 21.

In 1929 both Kalmia and Adam visited Dornach and met Ita Wegman. After a year or two working at Sunfield Children's Home in Clent near Stourbridge (the first anthroposophical home for children with special needs in Britain), Kalmia worked in Switzerland with Dr Wegman at the Sonnenhof children's home. She went back to Britain for a visit in 1940, but the German invasion of France made it impossible to return to Switzerland.

A chance meeting with one of the priests in London led her to renew her connection to '1001', where she had often been with her brother. The first Act of Consecration she attended was a special service on hearing of the ban of The Christian Community in Germany. She felt the responsibility resting on the small group of priests in Britain who were left to carry the great ideals of this religious movement, and this led to her resolve to become a priest.

After her ordination in October 1944 she was assigned to Leeds to take up the work that had been started by Oliver Mathews and by her brother. Here her social and educational ideals found a stage to work on.

3. WARTIME AND POSTWAR YEARS

Kalmia Bittleston

Kalmia lived in what she euphemistically called the 'cottage', which was, in fact, a barely metamorphosed washhouse. There were Latvian refugees, there was the beginning of a Waldorf school initiative. And then there were the unexpected local children turning up at the door saying, 'We've nowt to do, Miss.'[7]

During this time a young social worker, Winifred Hunt, came to live in the house, leading to a lifelong friendship. Kalmia was asked to move to London in 1953. She and Winifred moved to Lewisham in south-east London, and Kalmia worked for six years in Temple Lodge, Hammersmith. After this time she helped out wherever needed, including a time of working in Kings Langley until she retired in 1979. Even after this she was always active, translating the gospels as well as taking up voluntary social work.

Michael Tapp characterised her particular relationship to those who had died:

Her great knowledge rarely came to the fore, but lay concealed in her matter-of-fact and highly practical approach to questions on all levels. She never seemed to wish the world to be other than it was: she accepted, not with resignation, but with understanding and with humour. All this was combined with what was perhaps the most important aspect of her life: communion with the dead. The community at whose centre she stood embraced both sides of the threshold and all those, whose names were noted throughout her long life, had a regular place in her inner life. Hers was a congregation that existed beyond a particular time and place. Accepting the human being and the world as they are is one thing. It is quite another to accept and live with a spiritual world as it is. Yet that was her double achievement, in a world that has difficulty in accepting either. Her life was a daily witness to the interweaving of the two worlds, indeed she was herself an instrument of this interweaving and for her, crossing the threshold will have been simply a move from one part of the community to another.[8]

Peter Roth
1914 March 12, Vienna –
1997 October 14, St Albans, Herts.

Peter's life as a priest and his life as one of the founders of Camphill are deeply intertwined and sometimes difficult to distinguish. He grew up in Vienna, the son of a well-to-do Jewish family and studied medicine with a view to becoming a psychotherapist. He was part of the anthroposophical youth group around Karl König until the *Anschluss*, Nazi Germany's invasion and annexation of Austria, put an end to his almost completed studies. In 1938 he managed to flee to London and later that year married Anke Nederhoed, another member of König's youth group. In March 1939 when Kirkton House, the forerunner of Camphill, was started by König and a number of Viennese refugees, Peter and Anke were there.

3. WARTIME AND POSTWAR YEARS

Peter Roth

Peter felt that behind his wish to become a psychotherapist lay the ideal of priesthood and pastoral medical work, and a recognition that his task was to work not as a physician but as a priest. Encouraged by his fellow Camphillers he embarked on a year's training in London and was ordained in 1944, working for another year with the congregation in London before returning to Camphill. In 1946 he became seriously ill with polio, leaving him disabled for the rest of his life.

Peter had a wonderfully warm heart and a tremendous ability to listen, but was sometimes clumsy in his ability to express his thoughts clearly, and became increasingly clumsy in his actions. Baruch Urieli characterised Peter:

> Already in the early years of the pioneering work in Scotland the contrast between Peter's keen observation of, and warm human relation to, fellow human beings and a naive and sometimes clumsy unworldliness began to show. It is told that Peter asked

once in astonishment why one should put good edible potatoes into the earth in spring if one anyway had to take them out again in autumn.[9]

His marriage to Anke ended (Anke later married Thomas Weihs). In 1953 he married Kate (Kathleen Elderton) and moved to Ringwood, a new Camphill venture in the south of England. Kate and Peter moved to Botton Village in Yorkshire when it started in 1955 as a Camphill centre for adults with learning disabilities. König's ideal was for these adults and their carers to live together as families, with workshops and village life that included a church. It was there that Peter took up celebrating services again after a break of seven years following his illness (though he was unable to celebrate the service anywhere where there were steps before the altar.)

Peter travelled a lot, particularly after König's death in 1966 when he took on a central role in the Camphill movement. In 1959 he visited South Africa, and was the first to celebrate the Act of Consecration of Man there.

Peter had a deep yearning for a unity of the Camphill movement, the Anthroposophical Society and The Christian Community, and often had difficulty distinguishing their roles. It took many meetings and a long time for Peter to see that membership of Camphill and of The Christian Community could not be identical. Tom Ravetz wrote:

> His life was lived in the service of Christ and he had a very priestly quality; I would however describe it as the quality of the priesthood of all believers, to which we should all aspire. He had no Christian heritage and was not at all 'churchy' ... he saw many people and offered a listening ear and guidance in many realms of life. These conversations were priestly in the sense that they were deeply genuine and Peter listened with openness and compassion to everyone who came. I remember asking him once in the early eighties about the Sacramental Consultation, and he told me he had hardly used this sacrament which would have added the specifically priestly element to his care of souls.

I am sure it was partly Peter's dual role which made this so; what also played a part was his deep conviction that all the anthroposophical daughter movements should be united, not only in individuals, but on an institutional level.[10]

In 1992 he moved to Delrow, a Camphill centre north of London, where he died in 1997.[11]

The immediate postwar

In September 1945 a conference took place near Shrewsbury – the first time since the war that it was possible to hire a house for such a purpose – and members and friends from all over England and Scotland took part. With the plight of refugees and the destruction of so many chapels and other Christian Community properties (including the seminary) in Germany, there was a strong wish to help with reconstruction. There was fund-raising to help reconstruct the seminary in Stuttgart. However, the only way for funds to be sent to Germany was through the Committee for Christian Reconstruction in Europe, a department of the World Council of Churches. Some kind of arrangement appears to have been made, because funds did make their way to Germany. The house in Glenilla Road provided office and staff for some of the interdenominational schemes to send food parcels to Germany.

Despite all the outward hardships and continuing rationing, there was a surge of activity. Two ministers from other denominations, Will Sawkins and Donald Perkins, were ordained together with Marcia Dodwell in June 1946. While travel was still restricted to and from Germany, preventing Bock from coming to London himself to hold the ordination, this time it was celebrated with the full knowledge and awareness of the central leadership.

Will Sawkins, known affectionately as Father William

William Sawkins
1886 December 23, Thorpe-le-Soken, Essex – 1962 January 5, Stroud

Will Sawkins was almost sixty years old when he was ordained in 1946. This made him the oldest among the priests in Britain, and he was known affectionately as Father William. He lived strongly in his feelings, but was also widely read and intelligent which, combined with his rich experience, made him a fascinating personality. His strongly pronounced features, his deep voice, his humour, humility and wide interests, and 'the whole humble nobility of his character' (as Heidenreich put it) made an impression on those who met him.

He left school at the age of fourteen entering the office of a surveyor and architect. As a young man he felt a calling and became a Methodist lay preacher. Sawkins wrote for religious journals and for the local press. When the headmaster of his old, much-loved school died, he wrote an appreciation for the local paper, signing it

3. WARTIME AND POSTWAR YEARS

'An Ex-Scholar'. This so moved the headmaster's widow and daughter that they tracked down the author, and so Sawkins met the girl who became his wife early in the First World War.

He went on to study theology – no easy matter for one who had left school so early – and was an army chaplain during the First World War. At the end of the war he returned to the regular ministry, serving in a number of congregations (Methodist ministers usually move every three years). However, he did not feel his inner needs were fully met there.

He was a voracious reader, and became a Freemason (celebrating the rituals), went on to the study of theosophy, and then joined a small group of Rosicrucians, led by a Dr Sullivan. It was he who said to William Sawkins, 'If you wish to go further, you must study Rudolf Steiner.' So he began to study anthroposophy. He had a congregation in Manchester during the Second World War. It was there, at an anthroposophical meeting, that he met Adam Bittleston and heard about The Christian Community. He soon met the group of priests in London, and it was not long before he decided to offer himself as a candidate for the priesthood.

After his ordination he had a brief period in Leeds with Kalmia Bittleston, then went to Sheffield, where he gradually built up a congregation.

> Not a small undertaking for a man who had played a leading part in an established church with everything provided, to begin at the beginning at the age of sixty, with no permanent residence, no established chapel. It meant also a partial separation from his family. Before the house in Upperthorpe [Sheffield] was purchased as a home for The Christian Community, he had celebrated the Act of Consecration of Man in thirteen different places.[12]

Well over seventy, he entered a period of semi-retirement at Woodford House in Keswick. There he had a stroke during Advent 1961, and in the twelve Holy Nights deteriorated rapidly. He celebrated his 75th birthday at Keswick. He was moved to the care of Dr Glas in Stroud, and passed away on the eve of Epiphany.[13]

Marcia Dodwell

Marcia Dodwell
*1901 September 18, Wolverhampton –
1964 April 3, Jerusalem*

Marcia Bradley's father died when she was six. Her mother, a headmistress of a girls' school was left to bring up three children. Marcia showed brilliance, winning an open scholarship to Oxford where she studied botany. At Oxford she met fellow student David Dodwell who on completing his degree went into the Indian civil service. Marcia followed him and they were married in India in 1924, where their three children were born.

On the return voyage Marcia met a lady who told her about Rudolf Steiner and his theories on education. The children then attended the New School in Streatham, London. In 1934 she came to an Act of Consecration of Man at 1001 Finchley Road, and soon made her house in Streatham available for services.

In 1946 she was ordained in London and then went to work in Birmingham where she remained until her death. Through the Dodwell's generosity The Christian Community was given the house in Harborne, Birmingham. From there Marcia also visited Rugby

3. WARTIME AND POSTWAR YEARS

and Ilkeston. Oliver Mathews, who for a time worked with Marcia in Birmingham, wrote:

> A modern industrial city is not the easiest place for pioneer Christian work, particularly Birmingham with its changing population. So many people have passed through this congregation, and how few have stayed. I was born in Birmingham, but I must confess that I never learned to love the place, and have always been glad to get away from it. I think Marcia Dodwell came to love Birmingham, not that she had any illusions about the materialism, the egotism, the frustration of any modern city, but she saw the thwarted human possibilities, the incipient virtues, which she would so gladly have helped to release and cultivate. There is little doubt that the burden of this task was one cause of her comparatively early death. She gave her life for the work in Birmingham.
>
> Marcia Dodwell combined in a remarkable way gentleness and strength, wisdom and faith ... To whatever she had decided was worthwhile doing, she brought every ounce of her strength. Her inner strength was at the disposal of those in need. To many who had lost belief in life and in themselves she brought a new confidence, to the doubting a new certainty, to the sick and bereaved comfort. Her knowledge – and it covered a very wide field – was no abstraction, but closely allied to her heart and will, so that she brought overflowing enthusiasm to all her interests. Her faith in the future of the work she had undertaken was unbounded and poured into all she undertook...
>
> Her knowledge of anthroposophy combined with her deep connection with the plant world enabled her to make a very helpful contribution to the understanding of the significance of the various substances used in the celebration of sacraments.[14]

In 1959 a visit to the Holy Land made a deep impression on Dodwell, and henceforth this theme took on importance in her life. She had spent her early married life in the East and then worked in the West. It seems that in her concern to find a bridge between

East and West she chose the place of her death to be in the middle. On Friday April 3, 1964, she had just arrived in Jerusalem on another visit. She took a walk in the refreshing 'air of the Holy Land' towards the Damascus Gate with her daughter. She suddenly gripped her daughter's arm, saying 'O Janet,' and collapsed. She was dead when she arrived at hospital. Her body was laid in the Anglican Cathedral of St George's near the Damascus Gate and was buried at the Anglican cemetery near Bethlehem.[15]

Donald Perkins
1903 April 27, Saffron Walden, Essex –
1992 January 29, Hapstead, Devon

Donald Perkins became a Nonconformist lay preacher in Northampton at the age of seventeen and went on to study theology in Bradford, and philosophy and psychology at Edinburgh. He became a minister in the Congregational Church in 1929, working in Lancashire and Whitby. He married Patti in 1933, and in 1938 his first son Michael was born. In 1939 he moved to Aberdeen where one of his members told him of lectures by Ernst Lehrs and Karl König.

This was a turning point in his life, and he became increasingly interested in anthroposophy. In 1945 he resigned from the Congregational Church, went through the compressed wartime training given by Alfred Heidenreich and others, and was ordained in 1946. After a brief spell at Albrighton Hall in Shropshire he returned to Aberdeen where he worked as priest from 1947. His wife, who had moved south during his training, did not move back to Aberdeen with him, and the marriage was later dissolved.

His contact with Camphill strengthened and from 1952 he moved to Newton Dee outside Aberdeen, which became a Camphill Village for adults with learning disabilities. He married Helga Pfretzschner in 1955 and his second son John was born in 1956. He served as priest in Newton Dee until 1970 and then for ten years in Botton Village. After the sudden death of Helga in 1980 he moved to

3. WARTIME AND POSTWAR YEARS

Donald Perkins

Hapstead (Camphill) Village in Devon where he worked to the age of 85 before retiring from duties.

Peter Button remembers:

> He was always full of enthusiasm and zest for life and had a rich sense of humour. He was an excellent pastor and helped many people. When he visited hospitals he did not only speak to the one he was visiting, but would talk to all the other people in the ward. He was a good administrator, and prepared all that he did thoroughly ... Careful preparation went into all the sacraments he celebrated, and also in the preparation for membership. Among the members he received during his Newton Dee time was Taco Bay ...
>
> He had a great love for the English language and a special interest in the works of Dickens. He gave lectures about these works, and eventually published his book, *Charles Dickens: A New Perspective* in 1982. He made an important contribution in bringing about awareness of the greatness of English literature in the places where he worked.

Albrighton Hall

Donald was a fisherman, and in later life he began painting and took up beekeeping. He gave lectures on bees, and also on ants and other insects. He was particularly interested in the community aspect of the working of bees and ants. He himself, from the time he went to Newton Dee, always worked in a Camphill community setting. He liked to have a family around him, and after his wife Helga died in 1980, the people he lived with in Hapstead became his family.[16]

Albrighton Hall and Woodford House

In 1946 Albrighton Hall in Shropshire was purchased. It was to be a conference house, 'headquarters' holiday home and – a brave venture to meet a postwar need – an adult education centre to provide a place where ex-servicemen could reorientate themselves towards a new future. Heidenreich called it 'The Great New Undertaking' and hoped it would 'put us on the map in a new part of England, and would

3. WARTIME AND POSTWAR YEARS

The chapel built later in Woodford House

Gisela von Wiser

allow us to work on an almost national scale.' Although he realised that 'the risk that the responsibilities involved are somewhat ahead of our general development.' The purchase cost was £12,000 (perhaps £1.5 million in 2016's money), and typically for Heidenreich's financial daring at the time, only £3,000 was in hand, a mortgage of £5,000 was being arranged, and 'a balance of £4,000 has to be found' – as the monthly journal at the time baldly summed it up.[17] This staggering sum for those austere times was raised as loans and gifts within four weeks.

The first conferences and family holidays took place within a few weeks of its purchase and for a time it became the administrative centre of the Community in Britain. In 1947 there was a big international youth conference where, for the first time since the war, young people from Germany and other parts of Europe came together in Britain.

However, after seven years, needs had changed and it proved too costly to keep up. In 1953 conferences were moved to Woodford

Woodford House

House, Keswick in the Lake District, and the 'headquarters' returned to London. Woodford House was a small commercial hotel, which was bought through loans. As well as being a conference centre for the Community it continued as a guest house, offering accommodation on the shores of Derwentwater with the mountains in the background. For many years Gisela von Wiser ran it. She was the daughter of Baroness von Wiser, one of the early members of the Community in Darmstadt, which Heimeran and Heidenreich visited from Frankfurt before coming to Britain. Many conferences took place at Woodford House during the thirty years it served as a centre of the Community, until in the early eighties it was no longer financially viable.

The fifties

In 1950 the Community spread to Birmingham (with Oliver Mathews and Marcia Dodwell), Aberdeen with Donald Perkins, Sheffield with Will Sawkins and Edinburgh with Adam Bittleston. Oliver Mathews eventually moved to Stourbridge where he lived for the rest of his life. Numerous other places were visited regularly for a time. It has been said that the Community followed the members who had been evacuated from London during the war.

The New School (the first Waldorf school in Britain) did not return to London after being evacuated to Minehead in Somerset during the war, but settled in a large mansion in Forest Row, and was renamed Michael Hall. This had a major impact on both the Community and anthroposophical activities in London, as families wanting a Waldorf education for their children moved away from London. This led to Stanley Drake moving to Sussex with his family, where for many years the Community was in nearby Ashurst Wood. This congregation grew to be the largest in Britain, and in 1993 a church was built in Forest Row itself.

During the 1950s three more priests joined the work in Britain. In 1951 Muriel Allen was ordained. After teaching in a girls' school in Nottingham for some years she had found her way to The Christian Community in London during the war years. In 1946

PIONEERS OF RELIGIOUS RENEWAL

The view across Derwentwater from Woodford House

A synod in 1956 or 1957 at Woodford House, Keswick
Standing (left to right): Adam Bittleston, William Davie, Oliver Mathews,
Alfred Heidenreich, Peter Roth, Stanley Drake, Donald Perkins
Seated: Kalmia Bittleston, Muriel Allen, Eileen Hersey, Marcia Dodwell

A synod in 1962 at Woodford House, Keswick
Standing (left to right): Michael Tapp, Marcia Dodwell, Kalmia Bittleston, George Klockner, Peter Roth, Peter Button, Peter Kändler, William Davie, Adam Bittleston, Irene Taylor, Ormond Edwards, Alfred Heidenreich, Taco Bay
Seated: Stanley Drake, Marta Heimeran, Oliver Mathews, Muriel Allen

Heidenreich invited her to train as a priest with Verner Hegg and Jan Dostal at Albrighton Hall, but while the men were ordained in 1947, Muriel stayed on as housekeeper. Later she attended the seminary in Stuttgart for a year before being ordained. She worked for many years in Aberdeen, and after Marcia Dodwell's death in 1964 she took on the work in Birmingham, until that congregation closed in 1973. For some years she was in Stroud before retiring to Simeon Care Home in Camphill, Aberdeen. She died in 2000 aged 94.

In 1956 William Davie was ordained and worked for most of his time in Sheffield. Michael Tapp was ordained in 1959 and began work in Bristol (see also Chapter 6 on Australia and New Zealand).

Muriel Allen

William Davie

Michael Tapp relaxing at the seminary in the late 1950s

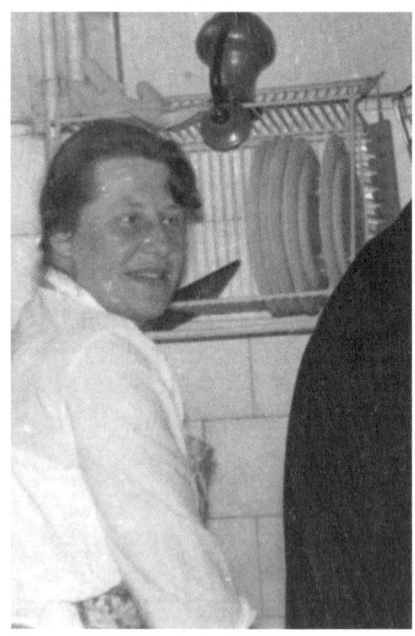
Ute Schobbert

The new church at Glenilla Road, London, 1949

London

In 1948 the first British Christian Community church was built on the site adjoining the social centre in Glenilla Road. The planning authorities deemed it a 'temporary' structure (which was to be demolished when The Christian Community no longer used it). The architect, Kenneth Bayes, a member of the congregation, did an admirable job of creating a church from prefabricated elements which looked anything but 'temporary'.

Evelyn Francis and Alfred Heidenreich were both larger than life personalities, but unfortunately that did not lead to a harmonious working relationship. Having helped acquire the new house in Glenilla Road in 1943 and built up its standing as a social centre, Evelyn was devastated when in 1951 she was asked to go to Bristol. She refused. This led to a rift in the London congregation, with many following Evelyn to west London where they eventually settled in Hammersmith. To Heidenreich's credit he gave this venture his blessing. And they continued to work together (provided they were not too close).

Ormond Edwards, ordained in 1960   *Irene Taylor, ordained in 1960, married Ormond Edwards in 1963*

Glenilla Road in its heyday had four or five priests, numerous activities, a large youth group which extended far beyond the congregation, concerts and exhibitions. It was also the 'headquarters' as Heidenreich liked to call it, with the journal and books published from there. Ute Schobbert the housekeeper deserves a special mention for keeping everything running.

Temple Lodge in Hammersmith was also a hive of activity with lectures, courses and many events. The building lent itself to offering accommodation, which over the years has been improved to become an excellent bed and breakfast. There was also a restaurant, a bookshop and soon its own publishing venture, Temple Lodge Publishing.

However, the difficult relationship between Alfred Heidenreich and Evelyn Francis was reflected in the congregations which, despite their relatively close proximity, had little to do with each other. The London West congregation was even a different legal entity from the congregations in the rest of the country.

Despite many attempts in the seventies and eighties to bring some kind of reconciliation and joint venture, this failed, and by the nineties both congregations, particularly Glenilla Road, had dwindled in size.

3. WARTIME AND POSTWAR YEARS

Temple Lodge, Hammersmith, London

Peter van Breda

In 2001 Peter van Breda came to be the priest for both congregations and worked tirelessly through a painful process that finally led to a single congregation, for a time with two altars. In 2009 the house in Glenilla Road was sold, and the bulk of the proceeds paid for a new church to be built in Hammersmith, which was completed in 2013. The new church is a beautiful quiet oasis – outside you hear the traffic from the Hammersmith flyover, the rattle of the underground and the continual low flying planes on their approach to Heathrow airport, but inside it is still. Soon after the consecration of the church the difficult and distressing decision was made to also sell the site of the church in Glenilla Road.

Camphill and The Christian Community

As the children with learning disabilities at Camphill School grew older, a need arose for adults to have a meaningful occupation in a caring environment. In 1954 Botton Village on the North Yorkshire Moors was established as the first Camphill village for adults with learning disabilities, developing what had been started in Newton Dee, Aberdeen in the late 1940s. Karl König saw it as a matter of course that the village should have a Christian Community with regular services. Peter Roth was priest in Botton, and when Newton Dee became a Village in 1961 Donald Perkins was priest there.

The strong links between various Camphill centres and The Christian Community both in Britain and in other countries (particularly South Africa) was not without problems, and for some it was difficult to distinguish the two movements. Peter Roth took many years to see that membership of Camphill and membership of The Christian Community were not identical. Taco Bay, who spent his early working life in Camphill before becoming a priest, also had difficulties in that direction, though he did much to clarify them when he became erzoberlenker. In the last few years in Britain, with government finances for Camphill being cut, and with many changes in the Camphill movement, this relationship is no longer as strong as it was.

3. WARTIME AND POSTWAR YEARS

Karl König, founder of Camphill *Peter Button*

The sixties and seventies

Heidenreich's responsibilities as oberlenker meant he was often in Germany for meetings, as well as being lenker for Britain and North America. In 1962 it was decided that Oliver Mathews should be lenker of Britain and Rudolf Koehler lenker for North America. In practice this did not make much difference in Britain, as Heidenreich, with all his vision, drive and energy was still regarded as the leader.

In 1962 Peter Button and Taco Bay were ordained in London. Peter joined Muriel Allen in Aberdeen, and Taco worked in Edinburgh with Adam Bittleston. This time was perhaps that of greatest outward expansion in Britain. As well as today's congregations with resident priests (apart from Devon) there were priests living in Leeds, Sheffield, Birmingham and Bristol, and other places like Corbridge (near Newcastle) and Shrewsbury were visited. Many conferences were held at Woodford House and elsewhere. Michael Tapp started summer youth camps, and as well as an annual summer youth conference there were weekends in different centres around the

A synod in 1966 at Glenilla Road, London (non priests in parentheses)
Very back (centre): Michael Tapp, Alfred Heidenreich (below), (–),
Very back (right): Peter Kändler, Peter Allan
Middle back: James Langbecker, Taco Bay, (Ute Schobbert), Eileen Hersey,
Kalmia Bittleston, (–), George Klockner, (–), Oliver Mathews,
Ormond Edwards, (–), Donald Perkins
Front: Stanley Drake, (–), (–), (Nimmo Allan), William Davie, Walter Brecker

A synod in 1982 or 1983 at Woodford House, Keswick
Standing (left to right): Evelyn Francis, Irene Taylor, David Wilmot,
Kalmia Bittleston, Ormond Edwards, Elke Baublies, William Davie,
Muriel Allen, Tammo von Freeden, Oliver Mathews, Louise Cais, Georg
Klockner, Douglas Thackray, Jon Madsen, Baruch Urieli, Michael Tapp
Seated/kneeling: Peter Button, Bill Boyd, Pearl Goodwin, Roger Druitt,
(Gisela von Wiser), Stanley Drake

country. A youth magazine, *The Fountain,* was produced for some years in the late 1960s, and Taco Bay started children's camps.

Twenty-one years after the first British church was built in London, in 1968 a modest church was built in Stroud. Michael Tapp, who had been visiting from Bristol, moved to Stroud, and this congregation began to grow, to the extent that now it needs to build a bigger church.

Taco Bay
1933 September 22, Beatenberg, Switzerland –
2011 August 5, Überlingen, Germany

Taco's father was Paul Bay, a Swiss architect who had worked up a number of Rudolf Steiner's designs for houses in Dornach. Taco's mother was Dutch, and he was born the last of seven children. In the late thirties Paul Bay was put in charge of refugee camps for the thousands who fled Nazi Germany to neutral Switzerland. There Taco went to several different schools and was taught in (Swiss) German, French, Italian and Dutch.

In 1947 the family moved to England where Paul Bay taught art at Hawkwood College, Stroud, which offered courses on different aspects of anthroposophy. Taco learned English, went to Wynstones School and would occasionally attend courses at Hawkwood, thus coming into contact with many renowned anthroposophists of the day, like Ernst Lehrs and Walter Johannes Stein. The family moved to Aberdeen to join Karl König's thriving Camphill community. Taco began working in Camphill at the age of sixteen, joining the seminary in curative education, which also involved a lot of practical work. After completing the course he left Camphill, taking various jobs in Switzerland to fund his intended medical studies. However, he was soon asked to return to Camphill to do building work with boys with behavioural problems, including designing and building the chapel in Newton Dee where Donald Perkins celebrated the services.

In 1956 he married Ita Meeder, a Dutch co-worker in Camphill, and they became house-parents for a group of boys with behavioural problems. Their first two children were born in Newton Dee.

Taco's relationship to the Act of Consecration of Man grew into a resolve to become a priest, and in 1959 he took his family to Stuttgart. However, he did not have an easy time there – arriving at the seminary with a family was unheard of in those days, and his qualities were not appreciated by the leaders of the seminary. In fact after two years they wrote to Alfred Heidenreich expressing their doubts about ordaining him, but leaving it open – if Heidenreich felt that Taco could be of use, to arrange his final training in Britain.[18] Taco completed his training in Forest Row with Stanley Drake and was ordained in London (together with Peter Button) in 1962.

> When Dr Frieling ... went through a rehearsal for the ordination the previous day, he found that his shoes squeaked. In order to solve the problem Taco gave him a pair of his shoes to wear. Later this role was reversed when he was asked to step into Dr Frieling's shoes.[19]

Taco worked in Edinburgh with Adam Bittleston, saw the move to a bigger house which still serves the congregation today, and built up children's work, including running the first Christian Community children's camp in Britain in 1963. Taco and Ita had three more children during this time in Edinburgh.

Taco always had time for people to see him, to talk with him and receive help with any problems. He was always positive – at times when others would have moaned or groaned, one felt he was almost relentlessly positive. He also began working for the Samaritans, a telephone service providing help to suicidal or desperate people, gaining a reputation there of working with particularly difficult cases.

In the early 1970s Taco was asked to go to Australia to help found The Christian Community there. Ita, his wife, had long thought about becoming a priest herself, so she went for training in order to work with Taco in Australia. She was ordained in Edinburgh in 1973.

3. WARTIME AND POSTWAR YEARS

Taco Bay and Ita Bay

But things do not always go as planned. In 1974, at the same time as Michael Tapp became lenker in Britain, Taco became lenker of the Netherlands, and soon afterwards the family moved to Zeist in Holland. This was for a fairly short time, for in 1977 Frieling designated Taco to be his successor as erzoberlenker. As this would mean eventually moving to Stuttgart, Taco felt it better to move immediately to be able to work more closely with Frieling and the other founding priests. For the first time someone who had not been one of the founders would lead The Christian Community. For the last six years of his life Frieling was ill and Taco carried out his duties. Then in 1986 on Frieling's death he became erzoberlenker.

It was not easy for Taco (and Ita) to work in Stuttgart. Many of their colleagues did not appreciate Taco's qualities – he had a big heart and social skills, but was not academic, and was sometimes stubborn and wilful, even to the point of bullying (charmingly, of course).

As the movement was growing internationally, one of the great steps taken by Taco was to separate out German responsibilities from worldwide responsibilities, and also to fully entrust the finances into the hands of non-priests. He initiated a new body with an English name, Foundation The Christian Community (international), which was to carry the central worldwide tasks of the movement.

To English ears the name may sound a little misleading in that it is not a foundation which has great sums of money to disperse largesse or make grants. Taco chose the name because at the heart of The Christian Community are the sacraments, and while priests have freedom in their teaching, the form and wording of the sacraments is fixed and cannot be arbitrarily altered. This is the foundation of the movement. The body responsible for ensuring that the sacraments are worthily celebrated is the Circle of Seven – the three oberlenkers and four lenkers. This new Foundation, to which all congregations contribute (usually through their region), was there to support this central tenet of the Community, and thus the name arose.

To express its worldwide task, all the papers, minutes and reports of the Foundation were written in English. However, more than three quarters of the worldwide movement is in Germany, and German is often the most practical language for international meetings, so today this principle is not kept as strictly as it was to begin with.

With a growing number of new priests from other countries, ordinations were held outside Germany, something that previously had been exceptional. As ordinations are generally held by the erzoberlenker, here Taco's early schooling in different languages came to the fore, for he held ordinations not only in German and English, but several times in Dutch and twice in French. Over 240 priests were ordained by Taco – more than any of his predecessors had ordained.

In 1989 there were severe problems at the seminary in Stuttgart, which were eventually resolved by establishing two other seminaries, one in Hamburg and the other in Chicago (which subsequently moved to Spring Valley, New York). Another great change was the move of leadership from Stuttgart to Berlin in 2005.

Taco's health had never been strong, and he never spared himself if he saw tasks ahead. In 1988 he became seriously ill with a heart condition and needed an operation and induced coma, from which he recovered and continued his work. In 2004 he needed another operation for a tumour at the base of his brain. Again he recovered and was able to work.

Probably the greatest change within the priests circle was Taco's decision to step down from being erzoberlenker, and hand over to his successor in 2005. Until then the erzoberlenker held the office until death, even if unable to carry out his tasks. (In this The Christian Community was ahead of the Roman Catholic Church: Pope Benedict XVI stepped down eight years later.) Taking this step consequently also meant handing back the vestment collar of office. This new stepping down was then also done by all retired lenkers and oberlenkers who until then had retained their vestments of office.

After retiring, Taco and Ita worked for a few years in New Zealand as congregational priests before returning to Germany where they lived at the Lake of Constance. He died on August 5, 2011. Ita, without whom he could not have carried out his life's work, died four years later on July 6, 2015.

As far as I know, Taco was the first person to receive and to give all seven sacraments (as generally only the erzoberlenker ordains, all previous erzoberlenkers had not been baptised in The Christian Community).[20]

Shalesbrook

One of Heidenreich's last great projects was Shalesbrook in Forest Row, a centre for training priests in English, which was established in 1967. Courses were run in association with Emerson College. James Langbecker, a newly ordained American priest who was working with Stanley Drake in Forest Row was asked to be resident priest at Shalesbrook. James was also an architect and do-it-yourself enthusiast, and contributed enormously to the practical conversion of this large house into student accommodation.

Shalesbrook

Francis Edmunds, founder of Emerson College, and Adam Bittleston

Adam Bittleston and Rudolf Koehler in Forest Row, 1969

3. WARTIME AND POSTWAR YEARS

Alfred Heidenreich in the last year of his life

Heidenreich's sudden death in 1969 made this new undertaking more challenging. Rudolf Koehler came from Toronto to take on the leadership of Shalesbrook, but in spring and summer would return to America. In September 1970 Adam Bittleston moved from Edinburgh to take on this role. A number of priests did some of their training there, going on to Stuttgart to finish it. A few, like Michael Jones and Ita Bay, did their complete training at Shalesbrook.

By 1981 Shalesbrook was stretching the resources of the Community in Britain, and it was decided to sell the house. The plan was to have a six-month introductory course in Britain before students went on to the seminary in Stuttgart to complete their training.

Only when the seminary in Chicago started in 2003 did it become possible again to do a good part of the training in English.

Ireland

In Ireland The Christian Community grew out of Camphill's work. The Glencraig Camphill community near Belfast was founded in 1954, and in 1956 Peter Roth was called for two christenings there. In the following years he came to Glencraig or Dublin whenever a special sacrament was asked for. It is not known whether he ever celebrated the Act of Consecration during his visits.

In 1967 Glencraig requested regular Christian Community services, and Taco Bay began visits from Edinburgh. When Mourne Grange was founded in 1971 as a second Camphill community in Ireland, it was included in Taco's visits. After Christmas 1975 Baruch Urieli moved to Glencraig from Edinburgh to become the first resident priest in Ireland, also making regular visits to Mourne Grange, and after 1979 to Duffcarrig in County Wexford in the Republic, as well as to Ballytobin, County Kilkenny from 1982. In 1986 Udo Steuck arrived at Mourne Grange as a second priest in Ireland, by which time Clanabogan near Omagh was also being visited. By 1988 a sixth Camphill centre, Dunshane in County Kildare, was being visited.

After twenty years of work within Camphill centres, a growing circle of friends had amassed outside Camphill, and the question of establishing a separate Christian Community centre arose. This led to the beginnings of The Christian Community in Holywood, near Belfast (pronounced like, but not to be confused with, the more glamorous Hollywood in California!) and by the early 1990s the Community had acquired a house there. Today, a priest lives in Holywood and from there visits Camphill centres in both Northern Ireland and parts of the Republic.

After twenty years of visits to the south, in 2003 during an all-Ireland conference at Epiphany it was decided that a centre to serve the Republic of Ireland should be set up in County Clare in the west. In late 2005 a house in Tuamgraney was acquired, and from 2009 until 2013 Malcolm Allsop was there as the first resident priest in the south of the island.

3. WARTIME AND POSTWAR YEARS

The first house of The Christian Community in Ireland, in Tuamgraney, Co Clare

Baruch Urieli around 1980, Udo Steuck

*Inside of the church in Stourbridge,
completed in 1988*

Consolidation

In 1974 Michael Tapp became lenker. At that time The Christian Community was stretched thinly in many places. Younger priests came, often with families, and as some of the older priests retired who had lived on a shoestring or had private means, it was necessary to become more realistic with finances. It was a time of consolidation, drawing together what had been started in the enthusiasm of the earlier years. Some painful choices had to be made, for example closing Woodford House, the conference centre in Keswick; closing Shalesbrook; and consolidating the places where priests were engaged to harbour limited resources. Michael laid the foundations for more transparent working amongst the priests, and also for the structure of The Christian Community in Britain as we have it today.

3. WARTIME AND POSTWAR YEARS

The church in Aberdeen

Muriel Allen, Peter Button, Maarten Udo de Haes, Ormond Edwards, Louise Madsen (née Cais) at the consecration of the church in Aberdeen

The church in Botton Village in the Yorkshire Moors

The entrance to the chapel at Canterbury

3. WARTIME AND POSTWAR YEARS

When in 1988 Michael moved to New Zealand, Louise Madsen (née Cais) became lenker. Ordained in 1977, Louise had worked for a time in Edinburgh and later in Stourbridge. In this time the consolidation of the previous decade began to show results. A new chapel was built in Stourbridge in 1988, replacing the wooden hut in Oliver Mathews' garden. For the first time a chapel was built in Britain that expressed something of the new religious sacraments that took place within it through its architecture. In the following years purpose-built, representative churches were built in Forest Row, Aberdeen and Botton Village, and more recently (2012) in Canterbury.

Christian Community Press and Floris Books

From the beginning of the work in England in 1929, booklets about the sacraments and other aspects of The Christian Community were produced on a donated mimeograph (stencil duplicator). Margaret Mitchell, one of the early members from Port Eynon in South Wales, was a dedicated helper, who translated and typed some of these early publications. Then in 1931, properly printed books and a journal were produced, as Heidenreich relates:

> One day a tall, bent, distinguished figure [appeared]... He was the Rev John Arthur Bell, Secretary and Superintendent of the Homes for Little Boys at Farningham, Kent. These Homes, the first cottage orphanage in England, were a remarkable institution. Boys were received at kindergarten age, would go to school on the premises until school-leaving age, and would then be offered a full training in one of the trade departments which were part of the Homes ... [including] a well-equipped printing shop.
> The Homes were not allowed to compete on the market, but in order to have practice material, they were free to print publications which would otherwise never be printed for lack of funds. Our publications qualified eminently under this rule, and so with the beginning of 1932 a printed Christian Community Journal began as a monthly magazine.[9]

A surprising number of books appeared in the following years, often first as monthly instalments which could then be bound into a single volume. Some of Rittelmeyer's books had been published by Macmillan in New York, and Heidenreich managed to buy the unsold stock of several hundred copies for a song.

In 1949 the publishing business was reconstructed as the Christian Community Press, and by 1976 there were about twenty religious titles in print. In that year it was decided to put the press onto a more professional footing – there was a recognition in Germany that if The Christian Community was to get its message into the world, it would have to be done in English, and financial capital was put into the English-language publishing to achieve this. The name was changed to Floris Books, and its task was to produce a wider range of books, which would make it easier to encourage bookshops to stock them.

Forty years ago I was asked to take on the work of publisher as a part-time job. Since then Floris has grown to having fourteen staff, producing over fifty new titles a year and having almost a thousand titles in print, ranging from wordless picture books to philosophical subjects that add to the cultural debate.

An overview today

In 2011 Tom Ravetz was made lenker in Britain and Ireland. Today (2016) there are sixteen full-time priests, five or six semi-retired ones, and half a dozen fully retired priests. The congregations stretch from Aberdeen in the north to Buckfastleigh, Devon, in the south, and from Canterbury in the east to County Clare in the west of Ireland. Some congregations are growing and thriving, a few are struggling, and others steadfastly hold their own. Overall the number of members and friends is probably not much different from what it was in the sixties and seventies.

3. WARTIME AND POSTWAR YEARS

Tom Ravetz

4.
Expansion to America

First visits

Just six years after the beginning of The Christian Community, priests visited North America in 1928. Hermann Groh, one of the founding priests, made a private trip of six months during which he also went to California. Unfortunately very little more is known of this visit.[1]

In August that year Wilhelm Hochweber, ordained in January, made a visit of almost a year to New York and Chicago. He had received an invitation before his ordination, and Rittelmeyer and Bock allowed him to visit and hold services if the opportunity arose. During that time he held services and talks in German. All three Christmas services were held, with some thirty people present, in Brooklyn at the home of Von Kellenbach, the German consul, who was an anthroposophist. (Some of those present still remembered the occasion fondly when The Christian Community finally came permanently to New York.) In January 1929 Hochweber was invited to Chicago by Dr Neovius, a prominent chiropractor. On arrival at Neovius' downtown office, he was almost caught up in a shooting between Al Capone gangsters and police (it was the time of prohibition). In Chicago he held weekly meetings. However, this visit did not lead to a longer-term founding of congregations.

It was many years later that things began to take shape. Heidenreich relates:

Towards the end of the war [1943–44] I received letters from a – to me – unknown American gentleman in which he pleaded

4. EXPANSION TO AMERICA

Wilhelm Hochweber in 1935

for the beginning of Christian Community activities in the United States and offered himself as a candidate for the priesthood. In those days all this seemed very far away. As I myself was cut off by war conditions from the other office-holders on the Continent who would have to have a say in the matter, I did not quite know what to do and, let it be confessed, never answered those letters. But Verner Hegg – this was the name of the gentleman – persevered and as soon as the war was over, he appeared in England. His is the historic merit of having taken the first real initiative towards bringing The Christian Community permanently to the United States.[2]

Adam Bittleston's visit

Verner Hegg finally received an answer in 1946, by which time he had formed a committee in New York to invite a priest to America. It was agreed that Adam Bittleston would come as soon as he was able to get a passage – in the months after the Second World War there was a severe shortage of shipping and thousands of American servicemen were returning home from Europe. In July he unexpectedly had the chance of flying to New York (something that took almost eighteen hours in those days), and was in North America for three months. In the eight days following his arrival all vestments and utensils for the service were prepared by two dedicated ladies in New York. Adam took part in an anthroposophical conference in Spring Valley, New York, and celebrated the service several times there. Here Verner Hegg experienced the Act of Consecration for the first time, and was so deeply moved that for several hours afterwards he could not speak. 'For me, it was an experience of the Grace of God, from the head to foot, an unseen, but deep-felt sunrise for the rest of the day – I knew for certain where I was to go and [what I was to] do.'[3]

During his time there Adam held more than thirty baptisms as well as five marriages and a funeral. In New York he held four weekly services in a rented room, sixteen floors up, looking over Broadway and Union Square. By the end of the period, the assembly had grown to almost a hundred people. As well as visiting Philadelphia, New Hampshire, Rhode Island and Boston, Adam was invited to California and spoke about The Christian Community to people in San Francisco, Sacramento and Los Angeles (the same cities in which there are congregations today). Before returning to Britain he visited Toronto and Montreal in Canada. On his return in October he was able to report that there was an earnest and definite demand for the movement in North America.

Verner Hegg
1906 November 20, Minneapolis, Minnesota –
1996 November 30, Spring Valley, New York

Verner Hegg has the distinction of having founded five new congregations during his almost fifty years of work as a priest.

He was brought up in the strict Swedish Mission Covenant Church, and after leaving home attended theological college in Chicago. There he married a fellow student, Dorothy Barackman

4. EXPANSION TO AMERICA

Verner Hegg, in the late 1940s

in 1929. On graduation in 1932 – in the midst of the Depression – he was sent to the Presbyterian Church in Colorado where their daughter Mary Ellen was born. Three weeks after this Dorothy died from complications in childbirth. Her mother took the baby to Minneapolis to care for her, and Verner did not see his daughter again for over thirty years.

He studied psychology in Minnesota. There was a brief marriage to Evelyn, which was soon annulled. For two years he taught agricultural economics to farmers, averaging some 3000 miles per month. At the age of 32 he became a Congregational minister in Tehachepi, California (north of Los Angeles). There the elderly librarian raised the question of reincarnation, which seemed plausible to him.

Soon afterwards he was offered a position at the New Thought Temple in Cincinnati where he met Dorothy Schlie. They married in 1940. At this time Verner was still searching for something more than had been offered in his theology studies. 'I hadn't lost Jesus the teacher, but Christ, the Risen One had faded away.'[4] Someone gave him a copy of Rom Landau's book, *God is My Adventure*. Landau described Rudolf Steiner as a leading spiritual figure of our time. A few days later Verner and Dorothy heard a lecture on anthroposophy by Friedrich Hiebel, then a Waldorf teacher in New York. Verner felt immediately 'He's got it!' though he could not quite define what 'it' was. Reading some books from the anthroposophical group in Cincinnati, Verner first came across The Christian Community.

When in 1942 his position at the temple was closed, Verner decided he would join the work of The Christian Community. He took various jobs to save up for his training, and wrote to London to enquire about priest's training (the letters which Heidenreich never got round to answering). Undaunted, he formed a sponsoring committee in New York to invite a priest to America, and this led to Adam Bittleston's visit in 1946.

Verner made it to London in November 1946 and was ordained a year later. After working in Britain for a few months, in August 1948 the Heggs returned to New York. Heidenreich followed in October, and by December The Christian Community in North America was officially founded.

In 1956 he went to California to found the congregations in Los Angeles and San Francisco practically at the same time, commuting between the two cities (some 400 miles).

In 1964 he divorced Dorothy and married Alstan Lippencott, the founder of Highland Hall Waldorf School in Los Angeles. Soon after this he made contact with his daughter (after thirty years), and at the age of 73 baptised his great-granddaughter.

Verner had visited Sacramento with increasing regularity from the early years in New York. In 1970 the congregation was incorporated, and they purchased and remodelled a church. From 1972 Friedrich Ogilvie was resident priest there, and Verner moved to Vancouver, Canada. There a house

Alstan and Verner Hegg, in 1964

4. EXPANSION TO AMERICA

was bought that could serve as a chapel and as priest's residence. Finally in 1978 Verner retired to Sacramento, helping in the congregation. He fully retired in 1990, and died in 1996 in Spring Valley.[5]

The first American priest

Verner Hegg was invited to London, and managed to get there in November 1946 (Dorothy followed some time later). They stayed with Evelyn Francis at the Community house in Glenilla Road and learned to serve. One day as he was at the rear of the church he noticed Heidenreich standing observing him. 'So you're the guy,' Heidenreich finally said. He had come from Albrighton Hall to meet 'this American'. Verner and Dorothy took part in the Community's life, but there was no formal training, and Verner became impatient, saying if they weren't going to do anything with him he would return to America.

In April 1947 Verner Hegg was sent to the train station in London to meet Emil Bock, arriving for his first visit to Britain since the war, and travelled with him to Albrighton Hall. After a meeting with the priests, Bock informed him that if all went well Hegg would be ordained in six months' time. This came as a surprise, but a short and intensive training followed at Albrighton Hall. Verner was ordained on December 7, 1947, in London by Alfred Heidenreich.

*Alfred Heidenreich, Emil Bock and
Gottfried Husemann at Albrighton Hall in 1947*

Verner Hegg, Josef Adamec, Alfred Heidenreich, Jan Dostal in Prague, December 1947

Prague

It is remarkable how the first beginnings in America in the west were interwoven with new beginnings in the east. Jan Dostal, who had been trained at Albrighton Hall (just before Verner), was to be ordained in Prague and help with the work there. After the Nazis banned The Christian Community in 1942 Josef Adamec had started work again in 1945, but he needed support. It was felt impossible so soon after the war for Bock to hold the ordination in German, so Heidenreich was to conduct the service in English a week after Verner Hegg's ordination. Heidenreich insisted that Hegg come to this event, and so Verner, Heidenreich and Evelyn Francis flew to Prague.

Tragically, in 1951 the Community was banned again, this time by the Communist government of Czechoslovakia. Adamec and Jan Dostal had to find work in Prague outside the Community. In 1968 during the Prague Spring, Adamec started work again – some two hundred people attended the service, all contacts he had kept alive during the years of the ban. But soon after the Soviet invasion later that year, it was banned for a third time. Adamec had a fourth beginning in 1990, and the Community now has four priests working there. Josef Adamec died in 1995; Jan Dostal died in 2015.

4. EXPANSION TO AMERICA

The first house of The Christian Community in the United States, at 309 West 74th Street, New York

Beginnings in New York

After working in Britain for a few months the Heggs returned to New York in August 1948, and Heidenreich followed them in October. It quickly became apparent that 'a visible permanent centre, which meant a house where we could create our own atmosphere and where a permanent address would provide a firm anchorage' was needed. But this was easier said than done.

In the two months between October and December, as well as numerous lectures and celebrations of the sacraments in a rented hall, about fifty properties (for both chapel and priest accommodation) were looked at, a legal non-profit corporation was formed, and finances were raised.

By British standards house prices in New York were astronomical. Nevertheless a five-storey house was found at 309 West 74th Street for $42,700 (£10,600 then). The house belonged to Duke Ellington, the jazz composer, and the main floor had five white baby grand pianos surrounded by ornate wall panelling. A great deal of conversion was needed to change it into a chapel. It was a typical 'Heidenreich model': a large house with the main floor used as a chapel and Community space, the priest living in the basement or attic, and the other floors rented out to bring the income needed to cover the loans. (The house in New York, together with the one in Edinburgh, are the only two remaining 'Heidenreich model' buildings, which still have a chapel, priest accommodation and rented floors to this day.)

However, finances were not so simple, as Heidenreich related:

> The financing of the purchase ... was the most nerve-racking and fantastic undertaking with which I have hitherto been associated. It gave me a deep insight into the economic life of America. It all comes down to this, that while the USA is at the moment the richest country in the world, and its banks carry astronomical sums, it is easier to borrow £1,000 in the UK than to borrow $50 in the USA ... It was a nasty shock to discover that it was practically impossible to raise a fair mortgage on our proposed property, as one could have done easily in the UK through the usual agencies of a building society or a bank. The cut-throat conditions offered by one or two banks who would consider the proposition at all left one simply gasping. It was not the individual banker or mortgage broker who was unobliging. On the contrary, they were individually very sympathetic. Some of them could not have been nicer. But they have to refer such matters to a committee, and their committee is underwritten by a committee in Philadelphia, and Philadelphia is underwritten by Washington, which is underwritten by Chicago, which is ... *ad infinitum*. I came to feel that one was dealing with a vast anonymous octopus, of which even leading financiers are but the servants – and victims.[6]

With barely half the purchasing sum in sight they went ahead, signed a contract and paid a deposit on this house. At the last moment Ann and Alfred Barnes were persuaded to make a large low-interest loan, and the house could be purchased. And on Saturday, December 11, 1948, the foundation of The Christian Community in North America took place. Before returning to Britain for Christmas, Heidenreich spent ten days in Canada, and Verner Hegg was left as sole pioneering priest in America. (In the same month as the founding in North America took place, so did the founding in France with Gerard Klockenbring in Strasbourg.)

In September of the following year Rudolf Frieling came to New York with his wife and worked there until 1954. Then in 1951 Frederick Burgevin joined them, but as Verner said, 'He had a hard time – he was still an Episcopalian priest.'[7]

Frederick Burgevin
1903 November 8, Kingston, New York –
1972 November 9 Arlesheim, Switzerland

Frederick Burgevin and his later wife Lavinia Sloan were at one of the first services held in a rented hall in New York in 1948 and came to a study group.

He was born one of ten children and after school worked in his father's horticultural business. Around the age of 21 he took a sudden interest in religion, studied language and literature at Columbia University, and then theology at the General Theological Seminary in New York City. On graduating in 1935 he worked as deacon and the priest in Brooklyn.

He felt his theological training was lacking and kept searching. When the United States entered the Second World War in 1942 he left the church and enlisted in the navy. During this time he married a woman in Scotland, but was divorced shortly afterwards. After the war he worked in various office jobs in New York.

In 1948 he met Lavinia Sloan, an anthroposophist who introduced him to Steiner's work. He was struck by its reality, and after meeting Heidenreich and The Christian Community, decided to offer himself for the priesthood. He sailed for Europe, and after a conference at Albrighton Hall went to the seminary in Stuttgart in 1949. There 'Fritz', as he was known, was a lone figure, a little aloof, and his fellow seminarists were surprised that he was to be ordained. (Neither Bock nor Husemann showed particular enthusiasm, but Heidenreich was

Frederick Burgevin

keen to have another priest in America.) After ordination in 1951 he was sent to New York, and married Lavinia Sloan.

He was an unremittingly striving soul and was deeply connected to the sacraments of the Community, but outwardly he appeared to remain rather Episcopalian. He did not find it easy working with Verner Hegg – the two were utterly different. And he did not seem to be able to work together with John Hunter who came to New York in 1955. He withdrew to Spring Valley, but soon his work with the Community fizzled out. His wife found him various paid positions, and he wrote a doctoral thesis about Nicholas of Cusa. When Lavinia died in the late sixties, he moved to Scotland, and had his work published – *Cribratia Alchrani: Nicholas Cusanun's Criticism of the Koran in the Light of his Philosophy of Religion.*

Around 1970, Margaret Lilienfeld, a faithful member from Spring Valley who had remained in contact with Burgevin, visited him in the south of England where she found him critically ill with cancer. She arranged for him to be treated at the Lukas Clinic in Arlesheim. Shortly before his death they were married, and she was at his side when he died.[8]

4. EXPANSION TO AMERICA

The East Coast

After Frieling returned to Germany, John Hunter came to New York in 1955 and worked for a year with Verner Hegg, who then left for California. Gregg Brewer joined John in New York until he went to work in the Copake Camphill village, about 100 miles north of New York City. Robert Patterson came in 1965 immediately after his ordination.

From New York City other places were visited. Spring Valley, New York is relatively close, and is now a centre with its own purpose-built church, resident priest and the American seminary. Robert Patterson visited Devon, near Philadelphia about 120 miles to the south, moved there in 1972 and within a few years a church was built. Washington D.C. was occasionally visited and today in Maryland there is a thriving congregation with two priests. In 1972 John Hunter moved to Boston, Massachusetts, where he had been visiting regularly. And in 1987 James Hindes moved from New York City to the Taconic Berkshire region to start a centre that had previously been occasionally visited. That too now has a beautiful purpose-built chapel in Hillsdale, New York State, just a few yards from Massachusetts.

The chapel in Devon, Pennsylvania

John Hunter

John Hunter
1917 October 29, Edinburgh –
1998 July 27, Lindenberg, Germany

John Hunter never lost his Scots accent in all his years in America. Gregg Brewer, who worked with him for eight years in New York, wrote, 'Many found John difficult. He had a Scots temperament, sometimes penurious, an attitude which extended beyond just money matters. Many did not see his generous side. I did.'[9]

John's father was a leading employee in an Edinburgh brewery who died when John was twelve. John had regularly attended the Church of Scotland then turned away from it. But around eighteen he received a strong religious impulse and a vision. He decided to study theology and become a minister.

At the beginning of the Second World War, aged 22, he refused military service as a conscientious objector. This alienated him from most of his friends, and was hard for him.

In 1940 he met George MacLeod, leader of the Iona Community, and met Alfred Heidenreich in 1942 at a conference on Iona, which Heidenreich and MacLeod had arranged. John easily took up anthroposophical ideas, but did not pursue them further.

John gave sermons on a probationary basis in the Church of Scotland from 1945 to 1947. During this time he arranged to go fishing with his friend, Duncan MacNeill, who was also a Presbyterian minister. Duncan turned up rather late, as he had to visit a person who was dying.

John asked, 'What do you say to a person in this situation?'

Duncan replied, 'I tell them about life after death, and perhaps even of a possible reincarnation.'

'How do you know about this?'

Duncan then told him that he'd been reading anthroposophy since 1938 and had known The Christian Community since 1941. (Duncan was a regular member in Edinburgh and died in 2012, aged 99). This led John to take a greater interest – he worked for a while in Camphill, Aberdeen – and in 1947 experienced the Act of Consecration of Man for the first time when Evelyn Francis visited Edinburgh. Here for the first time John felt, 'That's it.'

John went to the seminary in Stuttgart in 1949 and was ordained in 1951 with Muriel Allen, Frederick Burgevin and Richard Lewis. After a short stay in London he was sent to New York where he worked for a brief time with Frieling and Verner Hegg, and then for many years with Gregg Brewer and later Robert Patterson. In Stuttgart he had met his future wife, Elisabeth Hoppe, a eurythmy student. They were married in New York in 1958.

In the 1960s he produced the monthly New York congregation programme, which included a brief reflection that he penned. Properly printed, it was by far the most professional looking programme of The Christian Community in the English-speaking world. Some of his writings were later collected and published in a volume, *Just for Today*.

In 1972 at the same time as he moved to Boston, he became lenker for North America and held this office for sixteen years until Robert Patterson assumed the task, and John and Elisabeth retired to the south of Germany. A year before he died he visited Iona again, bringing alive memories of his original religious point of departure.[10]

Chicago

Having visited Chicago briefly in 1949, Heidenreich came again the following year to look towards founding a Community there. Gregg Brewer, the second American priest, had been ordained in Stuttgart at the end of 1949, and Heidenreich envisioned him working in Chicago. Heidenreich felt a sense of urgency. It was an ominous time in world affairs – the cold war was threatening to become a hot war sparked by hostilities in Korea.

> The overriding need of the hour is to underpin and strengthen the vision of every man's immortal value and the intrinsic moral nature of our universe. Progress on this moral front weighs heavier in the scales of ultimate decision than tanks or atom bombs.
> Here ... The Christian Community makes available great sources of divine revelation and divine powers ... Not for nothing have the gods given to the new form of the Mass the sacred name Act of Consecration of Man ... It is a living oracle of divine social inspiration in our midst. It is, therefore, a case for much gratitude that we have been able to open a second American missionary centre in Chicago, in the teeth of the threats of war.[11]

In April 1950 Heidenreich, having just been on a flying visit to Chicago, met Gregg Brewer and his family in New York. Filled with enthusiasm, he told Gregg of a 'likely' house, albeit a bit dilapidated, that had 'possibilities'. It was in fact the only affordable one they could find when they went there together. With a great deal of work and knocking out a wall, this house at 1409 North Dearborn Parkway (since sold) was transformed from a run-down building into something that could serve a congregation with a chapel and priest's accommodation. The Christian Community in Chicago was opened on December 7–8, 1950.

After the grand opening, Heidenreich departed for Britain, leaving Gregg to get on with it. The plan was for Rudolf Koehler to come and join Gregg in Chicago, but Koehler could not get a work visa for the United States. Instead in the fall of 1952 Rosemarie Bergmann came, and then Richard Lewis with his wife. Preparations had not been as thorough as in New York, and all three priests had to take outside jobs to make ends meet. Gregg also continued doing an inordinate amount of renovations, which were necessary around the large house.

In 1956 Gregg Brewer was sent to New York and five years later Richard Lewis was sent to San Francisco (when Verner Hegg went to Los Angeles). Rosemarie Bergmann was left on her own, and valiantly soldiered on for many years, helped occasionally by Rudolf Koehler from Toronto. She regularly visited (by bus) a rural centre near Milwaukee, Wisconsin, and visited Detroit, laying the foundations for Hartmut Junge to open a centre in the 'Motor City' in 1986.

The present church in Chicago was purchased and renovated in 1997 while Oliver Steinrueck was priest in Chicago.

Gregg Brewer
1922 September 17, Beverly, Massachusetts –
2003 June 23, Falmouth, Massachusetts

Gregg Brewer was born on the day after the founding of The Christian Community. At the age of five the family moved from Beverly by the sea inland to Reading. Soon there was another move to Queens, New York for some years before returning to Reading where he finished school. It was in that last year of school that he met Richard Lewis and they became firm friends.

The both went to Bowdoin College in Brunswick, Maine. They found in Professor Fritz Koelln an inspiring teacher of German. Gregg had always had a bit of a lackadaisical attitude to school and study, and one day he admitted in class, 'I'm not prepared today, sir.' Fritz Koelln looked into his little book and said, 'Mr Brewer, you were not prepared today, nor were you last time I called on you, or the time before that ... I'm going to have to flunk you in this course.' That seems to have prodded Gregg into action, for he studied hard and did very well after that.

Through Fritz, Gregg heard of anthroposophy and Rudolf Steiner, and started reading a book the professor gave him. Gregg had always had a feeling at Sunday school that his teachers didn't know what was really in the Bible; but with Fritz Koelln he felt he had met someone with insight. However, studies were interrupted when the United States entered the war, and Gregg was called up and served in the Pacific. Throughout the war he took Rittelmeyer's book *Meditation* with him. On being discharged, he resumed his studies at Bowdoin College and soon after became a member of the Anthroposophical Society.

During this time a fellow student set him up on a blind date. Shortly before he met her, he knew, 'I'm going to marry this Natalie.' Amazingly that is what happened, though it took a couple of years.

Richard Lewis, who had also returned to Bowdoin, concocted a plan to go to Europe – Richard wanted to go into the diplomatic service, and Gregg thought it might help him get a post teaching German at college level.

They managed to find a ship to Europe and got to Zurich in July 1947. Once there, Gregg set off immediately to Dornach, where he saw a performance of *Faust*, and decided to write his dissertation about Goethe's great work. Wanting to read Steiner's lectures on *Faust*, he found they were out of print, but someone suggested asking Rudolf Meyer, the priest in Zurich. When they first arrived in Zurich they had walked past a building with a sign saying '*Die Christengemeinschaft*', and Gregg thought that must be what Fritz Koelln had been talking about when describing different activities coming out of Steiner's work. So he went along and was invited to Wednesday night lectures, and soon also went to the youth group.

On Christmas Day, during a lonely walk on the hill above the city, it suddenly came to him that he should be a priest in The Christian Community. He had never been to a service, only to lectures. But as he related later, 'On very important things I made quick decisions.'[12]

In August 1948 Natalie came over from America to marry Gregg in The Christian Community in Zurich. He wanted to see whether

4. EXPANSION TO AMERICA

*Richard Lewis, Natalie and Gregg Brewer,
Fritz Koelln at the Brewers' wedding*

she could live with the idea that he should become a priest. In April 1949 they went to Stuttgart for Gregg to study at the seminary. There he met Heidenreich who had just returned from the founding in New York. Heidenreich had plans – he saw Gregg working in Chicago with an experienced priest (Rudolf Koehler was going to London to perfect his English in preparation). So Gregg had a short and intense time at the seminary, and was ordained in November 1949.

Just before that, in September, their son John Michael was born. Gottfried Husemann referred to him as the 'first seminary baby'. After a few months in Stuttgart as a congregational priest they returned to America via London. Gregg went to Chicago in April 1950, and as soon as the house was habitable fetched Natalie and the baby, who had been staying with relatives on the east coast.

After six years with the tiny congregation in Chicago, Gregg was sent to New York to work with John Hunter. From there he sometimes visited Copake Camphill village in upstate New York for

Gregg Brewer in 1968

weddings and christenings. When around 1964 he became ill with Hodgkin's disease he was sent to Copake, where they welcomed a priest, but didn't really expect him to last more than six months. However, Gregg 'refused to die'. His health went up and down. At times he was ill and had to go away for treatment. At other times he held services in Copake, did finance work for Copake, and also worked on setting up a central fund of The Christian Community in North America. He even started to build a congregation outside the Camphill village – the beginnings of the congregation in the Taconic Berkshire region.

In 1985 he returned to Chicago, again working there as one of three priests with Rosemarie Bergmann and Robert Patterson, but was often troubled with asthma. Finally, at the age of 72, in 1994 he retired to Cape Cod in Massachusetts where he died in 2003.[13]

4. EXPANSION TO AMERICA

Richard Lewis
1922 Oct 23, Reading, Massachusetts

Born as the youngest of five children, Richard Lewis grew up in Massachusetts. At the age of seventeen he got to know Gregg Brewer and they became close friends. After an extra postgraduate year at school he went to Bowdoin College in Maine to study chemistry, but after a year couldn't stand the way chemistry was being presented. During that time he took part in Professor Fritz Koelln's *Faust* course. Koelln had his students study Steiner's *Goethe's Conception of the World*. Richard said, 'With difficulty I read thirty or forty pages and gave it up – the man spoke as though you knew Plato and Aristotle personally; that was too much for me.'[14]

In 1943 his studies were interrupted when he was called into the navy, became an officer and trained for amphibious landings. He served in the Marshall Islands, Okinawa, and after the Japanese surrender, in Tokyo. In 1946, a few months before demobilisation, he was made captain. Home again, he met up with Gregg and Fritz Koelln, decided to become a diplomat and finish his studies by majoring in German. Gregg took up anthroposophy but Richard held back. They decided to study in Europe for a time, and got a place in Zurich, arriving there in the summer of 1947.

Some months later Gregg started going to Christian Community youth-group meetings and tried to interest Richard in it, but he would have none of it. As a subject for his dissertation he chose the poet Christian Morgenstern (despite it being Gregg's suggestion). To further his research, Gregg suggested he should meet the world's leading expert on Morgenstern.

'Who's that?'

'Rudolf Meyer, who lives just up the hill.'

'And who's he?'

'He wrote Morgenstern's biography; he's a priest of The Christian Community.'

To Richard that was like waving a red flag in front of a bull. But with

Richard Lewis in 1978

some trepidation he went to meet Meyer. He was welcomed and was never asked about his church attendance or offered to view the chapel. Then early in 1948 the American students in Zurich were invited to attend a performance of some of Hans Sachs's short plays – which took place at The Christian Community. As it was a literary event, Richard felt it could do no harm. Seeing the performance and the audience made him realise he had nothing to fear from these people, and so he began going to the youth group and even attending the service that Gregg had told him about.

With postwar rationing in Germany it was extremely difficult to get a visa to go there, but in summer 1948, having obtained a transit visa through Germany ostensibly to visit Sweden, Richard simply got off the train in Stuttgart to take part in an anthroposophical students' conference. He also met a number of Christian Community priests and was shown around the seminary. There he was able to be present at an ordination. Until then he had only seen three priests in vestments at once; now, as the music started, the priests began to come in: one, two, eight, thirty, fifty. This event made a deep impression on him. He interrupted his time in Stuttgart to return to Zurich for Gregg and Natalie Brewer's wedding. (How he managed to talk his way back into Germany with only a one-time transit visa is unclear, but says something about his diplomatic powers of persuasion.)

Back in Zurich, over the next few months his experiences matured into a firm decision to go to the seminary. In the youth group, to which he continued going, he met Tamara Mangold, and early in 1949 they became engaged. In April he travelled to Stuttgart together with Gregg and Natalie Brewer, and began studies at the seminary.

Richard was ordained in August 1951 and spent a few months working in England. In January 1952 he married Tamara, and in November they arrived in Chicago, joining the Brewers again.

He remained in Chicago, occasionally helping out in New York or Toronto, until 1961 when he was sent to California. He worked first in San Francisco for a couple of years, before ten years in Los Angeles until 1973. Since then he has been in Sacramento. He was one of the founders of what became Rudolf Steiner College in 1976.

Still in Sacramento, he retired in 2003 at the age of eighty. Ever active, he has gathered a vast amount of material on the history of The Christian Community in North America.[15]

Rosemarie Bergmann
1921 December 4, Chemnitz, Germany –
2011 September 27, Chicago

Rosemarie Bergmann is one of the few priests to have worked her entire life since ordination in one congregation. A friend called her the 'Angel of Chicago'. She was headstrong, even a zealot. Daniel Adcock characterised her from his time working with her:

> Rosemarie always left a very strong impression on all those who knew her. Her upright figure, black hair, beady sparkling eyes, her cheerful smile and her firm handshake. Rosemarie didn't mince her words and was very outspoken and direct when giving advice, encouragement and comfort to others.[15]

A synod in Chicago around 1984 or 1985
From back, left to right: Richard Dancey, Gisela Wielki, Werner Grimm, John Hunter, Diethart Jaehnig, Robert Patterson, Phillip Nusbaum, Walter Brecker, Richard Lewis, Rosesmarie Bergmann, James Hindes, Hartmut Junge, Gregg Brewer

Rosemarie was born as the eldest of four. Both her parents worked and she said of her early childhood that she grew up 'trained in freedom'. She was deeply disappointed by the Protestant religion lessons she received, and after confirmation left the church. She had similar experiences with Catholic religion lessons.

In 1940 she was drafted into *Reichsarbeitsdienst*, the Nazi labour service on farms. She managed to arrange a break to catch up with her *Abitur*, her end-of-school exams. By chance she found she could do this at the Rudolf Steiner School in Dresden (the only Waldorf school in Germany at the time that was still allowed to function). When she refused to give political lessons as leader of the labour service, she was transferred to an anti-aircraft unit.

After the war she went to Stuttgart and for the first time experienced the Act of Consecration. She left feeling it was something deeply familiar and at the same time lofty and distant. It was the fulfilment of everything she had been searching for, and she decided that her

4. EXPANSION TO AMERICA

Rudolf Koehler

task was to work in this movement. Before going to the seminary she worked with children in need of special care and helped in Karl Schubert's school for children with learning difficulties.

She was ordained in 1952. Shortly before her ordination she was awarded an immigration visa to the United States to look after a relative (her mother was German-American). On the strength of this she was assigned to Chicago. Gregg and Richard knew Rosemarie slightly from the seminary, and hadn't particularly liked her. Gregg remembers:

> So I wrote a rather sharp letter to Emil Bock. The tone of Dr Bock's reply was, in view of the tone of mine to him, remarkably calm and kind. In effect he said: 'Calm yourself, if you can't get on with her, send her back.' (At the same time Bock was telling her something like: 'If you can't stand it over there, come back. We'll find a place for you.')[16]

When Rosemarie arrived in August 1952, the Lewis family and the Brewers were on a much needed vacation. So Rosemarie's welcome to Chicago was a note from Gregg: 'Welcome to Chicago.

A North American synod at Copake, New York in 1978
Standing (left to right): Diethart Jaehnig, Gisela Wielki, James Langbecker, John Hunter, Ita Bay (visiting), Gregg Brewer, Werner Grimm, Erk Ludwig, Rosemarie Bergmann, Hartmut Junge
Seated: Taco Bay (visiting), Richard Lewis, Robert Patterson, Phillip Nusbaum, Walter Brecker, James Hindes

Verner Hegg, on his way to and from Minneapolis, will hold the Act of Consecration here on the 10th and the 24th. If you feel you can do it in English, please hold the Act of Consecration on the 17th and the 31st. We will be back on September 1st.'

She found a place working with a family as an au pair (all the priests in Chicago had outside jobs then). She ended her working week on Fridays, and then came into the city to work as a priest. By the end of 1952 a strange, almost miraculous transformation took place – the three priests, each very different, not only got on but learned from each other, and over the next four years held their own 'post-ordination seminar'.

4. EXPANSION TO AMERICA

In the mid fifties, after her two colleagues left, Rosemarie continued in Chicago on her own for 25 years, occasionally helped out by visits from Rudolf Koehler from Toronto.

She was finally joined by a succession of colleagues in the 1980s. She died in 2011.[17]

Canada

Adam Bittleston had briefly visited Toronto and Montreal in 1946, and Heidenreich visited for ten days at the end of 1948. After that Verner Hegg visited Toronto occasionally from New York. But when Rudolf Koehler arrived in Toronto in 1953 there was only a handful of people in the congregation – hardly enough to support a priest. However, Koehler was a true pioneer, used to financial hardship, and after a few years of strenuous and enthusiastic work he opened a church in a busy area as well as making regular visits to groups of supporters in Ottawa and Montreal.

By 1956 a second priest from Europe, Werner Grimm, could join him, and nine years later, Udo Lindenmeyer, a member of the congregation who trained at the seminary, returned as a priest. This freed Koehler for his wider task as lenker for North America. (In 1962 Heidenreich's lenker area was divided with Oliver Mathews responsible for Britain and Rudolf Koehler for North America, allowing Heidenreich to concentrate on his responsibilities as oberlenker.)

Later, in the 1970s, Rudolf Koehler returned to Europe as oberlenker, with John Hunter taking on responsibility for North America. Udo Lindenmeyer also returned to Europe, leaving Werner Grimm alone in Canada until he was joined by Hartmut Junge in 1975 and by Phillip Nusbaum in 1978.

Today the congregation in Toronto has its own purpose-built church, and regular visits are made to Ottawa (over 400 km to the east), Durham (150 km to the north-west), to the Camphill community north of Toronto and to Montreal.

The house of The Christian Community in North Hollywood, Los Angeles

The West

As well as Adam Bittleston's visit to California in 1946, both Verner Hegg and Rudolf Frieling visited from New York, with Verner developing wide contacts on the west coast. In 1956 Verner left New York and began working simultaneously in Los Angeles and San Francisco, travelling 400 miles each way in an ancient car. Within a few years he had houses and chapels in each city.

Richard Lewis described the two cities:[18] San Francisco is on a peninsula with the bay on one side, hot springs to the north, and the Pacific with the cold Alaska current on the other side. It is on a fault line producing earthquakes. But the people were conservative and down-to-earth. It is like an over-abundance of life with a veneer of hardness. Los Angeles by contrast, is in a dry area, mile upon mile of oil pumps down Long Beach. The palm trees with their shallow roots, long trunk and then a burst of green creating an illusion of lush vegetation, like the illusionary world of films. A dry hardness with a veneer of vigorous life.

4. EXPANSION TO AMERICA

A synod in 1979 in Sacramento
Standing (left to right): Carl Stegmann, Werner Grimm, Walter Brecker, Taco Bay (visiting), Erk Ludwig, John Hunter (and Ita Bay hiding behind him), James Langbecker, Verner Hegg
Kneeling: Diethart Jaehnig, Richard Lewis

Verner's wife Dorothy, who had supported the work of the Community through many years, trained for the priesthood with Rudolf Koehler and was ordained in Toronto in 1961, the first ordination in America. After a time working in Toronto, she went to work in Los Angeles with Verner while Richard Lewis was assigned to San Francisco. However, Verner was in the process of divorcing her, and this led to difficulties in the congregation. Dorothy was asked to stop working in the congregation, and Verner moved to San Francisco with Richard coming to Los Angeles.

Ever on the lookout for new opportunities, Verner travelled north to Vancouver in Canada, gathering a congregation there. At the same time he was visiting Sacramento (merely 100 miles away in comparison to the 1000 miles to Vancouver). By 1970 the Sacramento congregation had found a suitable church, and in the following year he moved to Vancouver to concentrate fully on his fifth newly-founded congregation.

Around the same time, the congregation in Denver, Colorado was founded by Diethart Jaehnig, who came with Stegmann's initiative.

Verner Hegg retired to Sacramento in 1979 and Werner Grimm moved to Vancouver, taking the significant step of acquiring a large church building there.

Today there are five congregations in the west of America with resident priests. From Vancouver, the only congregation in western Canada, regular visits are made to Duncan on Vancouver Island and to Seattle, Washington, as well as occasional trips to Edmonton (800 km east) or to Hawaii (3500 km across the Pacific). From Sacramento visits are made to Santa Rosa, California, and to Eugene and Portland in Oregon. From San Francisco Santa Cruz is visited. The Los Angeles congregation still has the same building in North Hollywood that Verner Hegg acquired; from there San Diego is visited. In Denver, Colorado, James Hindes also visits Albuquerque and Santa Fe in New Mexico.

Stegmann's 'American Action'

In the late 1960s Carl Stegmann, one of the founding priests, visited his daughter in Oakland, California. It was the time following 'flower power' in San Francisco and student protests across the bay in Berkeley. He felt that a concerted effort from The Christian Community (at least a dozen priests) in the Bay Area would have far-reaching effects for the future of the continent. With great enthusiasm he held lectures and raised funds in Germany, and found some younger priests to go to America. However, there was little discussion or coordination with the priests in North America, who watched this development from afar with bemusement and misgivings. John Hunter and Verner Hegg voiced their concerns to the oberlenkers in Stuttgart. At this stage the momentum was too great to stop, and the American priests adopted an attitude of wait-and-see; if some of the new priests stayed and worked in the United States, it might be a good thing.

Together with five younger priests from Germany and Holland, at

4. EXPANSION TO AMERICA

Carl Stegmann

The church in Denver, Colorado

the age of 73 Stegmann moved to Oakland, California in 1970–71. After a time in Oakland, the young priests began to move out. Friedrich Ogilvie went to Sacramento for some years. They had just acquired a new church, and it was not an easy time. Erk Ludwig took over Verner's work in San Francisco.

Diethart Jaehnig went to Denver, Colorado, to found a congregation. After some years a church was built there with considerable financial help from friends in Europe; many young people from Europe and North America came to work on the building. Wolfgang Gädeke returned to Germany. Gisela Wielki also came to New York in the wake of the 'Action'.

The younger priests introduced more work with children and young people through summer camps and conferences, which have continued. Diethart Jaehnig organised the *Rethink* conferences, which drew many people to The Christian Community. In hindsight the America Action did not produce immediate far-reaching effects, but in an indirect way it did result in an overall growth in the movement in North America. It also encouraged greater collaboration between priests. Until then, the congregations were distant from each other, not only in miles, but also in outlook. Conferences took place, drawing people from all over the continent, and more recently North–South America conferences have been held every two years, alternating in location between North and South America.

The American seminary

In 2003 Gisela Wielki, who had been working in New York, started a seminary in Chicago. Since Shalesbrook closed in 1981, the only place to train for the priesthood was the seminary in Stuttgart, which posed a language barrier for English-speaking students. Chicago now offered some help before completing training in Germany. In 2011 the American seminary moved to Spring Valley, New York, and now offers training right through to ordination.

4. EXPANSION TO AMERICA

Translation

George Bernard Shaw observed that Britain and America were two countries divided by a common language. When the Community first began working in North America the rituals were celebrated in the same translation as used in Britain. From time to time parts of the original 1929 translation have been revised. The British version sometimes sounds old-fashioned or even archaic to American ears. For many years attempts were made by a group of priests from both sides of the Atlantic to find a common translation that satisfied these different peoples. This was a frustrating process. Peter Skaller, one of the Americans, commented, 'I worked for years through heated discussions on translation issues together with British colleagues where we all tore our hair out! (Lovingly, of course.)'[19] In the end they agreed to disagree, and now each region (North America, Britain and Ireland, Australia and New Zealand, Southern Africa) has its own translation.

Walter Brecker
1913/18 January 31, Johannesburg, South Africa –
1990 November 29, Los Angeles

Walter Brecker was full of contradictions. I struggled to decide whether he should go into the America chapter (where he worked for a time) or the South Africa chapter (where he was born), but I'm certain that this colourful character must not be omitted.

Walter was the first South African to be ordained. He could at times be loveable and charming, but at times could be quite mischievous and difficult for his colleagues to work with. John Hunter wrote:

> It was practically impossible to be angry with him. You always knew that tomorrow at latest he would make it up, and all would

sail forward smoothly again as if never a stormy breeze had ruffled the sails. I think that this side of Walter's life, both public and private, was such an essential part of Walter that neither his work nor his person can really be appreciated without taking it fully into account.[20]

It is not even clear when he was born. Both his own and official records show 1913, 1914 or 1918 as the year of his birth. His grandfather was German, his grandmother and mother were of mixed race. He had two brothers and two sisters. His family was divided by race under South Africa's apartheid laws – his brothers went to a mixed-race school, Walter and his sisters to a European school. 'Life was complicated and difficult,' he wrote.[21]

He worked as a fitter in an engineering firm, and at the outbreak of the Second World War joined the South African Air Force as ground staff, serving in Africa and in Europe. After demobilisation in 1947 he returned to Johannesburg, again working in an engineering firm where he eventually became plant manager. He became interested in social work. In 1957 he met Karl König and heard about anthroposophy. He went to Camphill in Scotland to attend the curative education seminar, and returned to South Africa in 1960, where he once more encountered the same problems of race.

He met Willem Zeylmans van Emmichoven (the lecturer and general secretary of the Anthroposophical Society in the Netherlands) on his last trip to South Africa in 1961. Zeylmans suggested that Walter should train at the priest seminary in Stuttgart. One day Walter turned up in Stuttgart at the seminary to be met by Alfred Heidenreich's son Michael, who opened the door for him. The seminary leaders were surprised to have Walter turn up on their doorstep out of the blue without having heard anything about him.

Alfred Heidenreich, who was beginning to see the possibility of The Christian Community taking root in South Africa, had hopes that Walter might be part of this. He was ordained in 1964 in London. However, in the meantime his citizenship in South Africa had been changed from 'White' to 'Coloured', which would preclude him

4. EXPANSION TO AMERICA

Walter Brecker in 1964

from ministering to Whites, and he would not be given a passport once he returned.

Instead Walter worked for a while in Bristol and Stourbridge, then in Botton Village, where he gradually stopped his priestly work. He busied himself in the Camphill candle workshop where he developed an apparatus for multiple candle-dipping. Rudolf Koehler persuaded him to resume his priestly task, and invited him to America.

For some time he worked in New York, and then from 1971 in Los Angeles after Richard Lewis went to Sacramento. His way of working was idiosyncratic – the programme was handwritten, adorned with his rather mystical poems. Besides his congregational activities he had a small workshop where he made candles that he sold, helping the Community finances, and – as he said – sending out more light into the world than any of his colleagues. His pastoral work, too, was unusual, often involving a quarrel, display of temperament, walking out, apparently totally breaking of relationships ... and then usually the next day things would be resolved.

In time Walter's health deteriorated, and in 1983 James Langbecker was assigned to work alongside him. John Hunter described the situation:

But unfortunately Walter had by then fallen into the illusion that he could 'go it alone' and needed no colleague. This he made quite plain to all concerned, and resolved secretly, in typical Walter style, to prevent the introduction of James to the congregation, which Patterson, Hunter and Langbecker had planned and arranged along with Walter ...

When the three priests turned up an hour before the introduction on Sunday morning, Walter was nowhere to be found. He lived next door to the chapel building but did not answer the doorbell or the telephone. Nor was his the only absence: with him had disappeared all that had been carefully prepared the previous evening – the chalice had disappeared and a goodly number of the necessary [vestments] ... In a frantic but controlled half-hour we found not very suitable but practicable alternatives, and the whole event went through as planned, without hitch and without comment and without Walter. It was actually quite a deadly thrust, and under other circumstances could have ruined the atmosphere for the occasion, if not the event itself. Fortunately James knew Walter well enough not to take offence. Whether any member of the congregation ever even heard of this escapade, I have no idea. In the evening of that day a somewhat disappointed Walter lifted the receiver and acknowledged that he had all the things safely at home. And so in a day or two everything was back to 'normal' again.[22]

In 1988 Walter managed to return to South Africa for the first time since his ordination. He turned down his South African colleagues' offer to join them as the apartheid era was over. He returned to Los Angeles instead, helped for a while in San Francisco and Santa Cruz, then lived for a time in Santa Fe, New Mexico. For a time no one knew where he lived. He was cared for in his last months by a devoted Community member in Los Angeles.

Despite all his temperamental quirks and oddities, Walter's reverence and devotion radiated from him, and made a deep impression on his congregation, and at his funeral the church was packed.[23]

4. EXPANSION TO AMERICA

South America

As a little digression, I would like to briefly mention a journey Heidenreich made in 1956 to Brazil and Argentina, which led to The Christian Community being founded there in 1960.

Günther Galle, a German priest, had visited Brazil in 1954, where there were groups of German-speaking members who had emigrated to that country at various times. He held services, baptisms and marriages, and also paid a brief visit to Argentina. In Buenos Aires a fairly large 'congregation' gathered, but so far did not have a priest. They had managed to form a financial basis and legal entity, La Communidad de Cristianos de la Argentina.

Heidenreich followed up on this visit two years later. It was quite clear to him that The Christian Community could not remain a monopoly of German-speakers. So he spent some time learning Spanish before going to South America, and the day after his arrival in Argentina began to take language classes to learn the local pronunciation. Together with Mr Habegger, a friend who had visited in London and invited him to come to Argentina, he began to translate the Act of Consecration. As well as holding public lectures in German and in English, at least twice a week he celebrated the Act of Consecration, usually in German, sometimes in English, and finally, at the end of his stay, in Spanish before a packed congregation.

One of the congregation, Erwin Kovacs, an émigré from Vienna, was so moved that he went on to seek ordination, and worked as a priest in Buenos Aires from 1960 until his death in 1975.

The contrast between Argentina and Brazil is great. Heidenreich described: 'Going to Brazil from the Argentine feels like going to Austria after Prussia.' Argentina is austere and demanding, Brazil inviting and forthcoming. The Portuguese spoken in Brazil is softer than the Spanish of Argentina.

In Brazil Heidenreich held services (in German) almost daily, a series of christenings, confirmations and a funeral, as well as giving public lectures (again in German).

Today there are Spanish-speaking congregations in Buenos Aires and in Plottier, Neuquén Province in the west of Argentina; in Lima, Peru; in Cali, Columbia, and visits to Santiago in Chile. In Portuguese-speaking Brazil there are congregations in São Paulo and Botucatu.

5.
Southern Africa

Priests had brought The Christian Community to Britain. The determination of one individual who later became a priest brought the work to North America. In Southern Africa the two founding priests were immigrants, both with strong links to Camphill.

First visits

Karl König visited South Africa in 1957, and soon after two Camphill schools for children were founded – Hermanus House in the Cape, and Cresset House between Johannesburg and Pretoria in the Transvaal. Among those working at Hermanus House were Julian Sleigh and Renate, Karl König's daughter. They wanted to get married and asked Peter Roth to come from England to hold their wedding service in 1959. Peter thus became the first to celebrate the Act of Consecration of Man in Africa on February 15, 1959.

After Evelyn Francis's husband Samuel Derry died, a friend suggested she take a holiday in South Africa. She visited in 1962, but Evelyn was not someone to put her feet up and relax. Her 'holiday' was filled with giving lectures, holding consultations and celebrating sacraments, building an extensive network of contacts. She visited again in 1963. Her main activities took place at the home of Heinz Maurer, who had also worked at Hermanus House and was then running a day-care centre for children with learning disabilities in Cape Town. She also visited groups of people in Port Elizabeth,

Evelyn Francis in South Africa

Ordination May 2, 1965, at Glenilla Road, London
Left to right: Rudolf Frieling, Udo Lindenmeyer, Robert Patterson, Julian Sleigh, Heinz Maurer, Alfred Heidenreich

Durban, Johannesburg, Pretoria and Salisbury in Rhodesia (now Harare, Zimbabwe). One can truly say that she laid the foundations of all the congregations in South Africa.

Heinz Maurer had begun training at the seminary in Stuttgart many years earlier, but life took him to South Africa. Now with Evelyn's encouragement, his wish to become a priest was reignited. Together with Julian Sleigh he went to the seminary in Stuttgart, and they were both ordained in London in 1965.

On Whitsunday, June 6, 1965 a founding festival was celebrated in Cape Town with Heinz Maurer and Julian Sleigh being introduced to their work by Alfred Heidenreich and Evelyn Francis. It was an unusual beginning, as there was not yet a group or congregation sufficiently strong to support two new priests and their families. A room in the Jan Prins Day-care Centre was prepared as a chapel and made available for the Community, and Heinz's wife Liselotte continued with curative work in the centre.

Heinz Maurer
1912 January 22, Stuttgart –
1982 June 22, Johannesburg

If Heinz had not been a priest, he would have been a born diplomat. He approached people easily, and was respected and welcomed in various groups – even those in conflict with each other – and often mediated.

Born in Stuttgart, he never lost his Swabian accent, even when speaking English. He first came into contact with The Christian Community while studying theology in Tübingen where he became involved in its youth group. Here he developed a friendship with a fellow student, Diether Lauenstein, who later became a priest and then retired to Windhoek, Namibia, where they met up again. After completing his studies he went to the seminary in Stuttgart in 1935. Emil Bock recommended he should have a break and seek some practical work. This break lasted 28 years.

Heinz Maurer

In 1947 he married Liselotte Storr, a nurse, and they had two children. They wanted to emigrate to South Africa to work in anthroposophical education for children with special needs. They worked at the Camphill community, Hermanus House in the Cape, and later they started a day centre in Cape Town. When Peter Roth came from England to hold the wedding service for Julian Sleigh and Renate König in 1959, he stayed with the Maurers. Evelyn Francis came in 1962 and 1963, and she too stayed with the Maurers in Cape Town.

Following Evelyn's visit serious preparations were being made towards permanently establishing the Community in South Africa, and there was a search for young people who might take the step of training for the priesthood. Heinz, then fifty years old, wrote:

Recognising the urgency of the situation and the needs of the circle of people in whose midst I found myself, it appeared to me to be right – after speaking to my wife and [to Evelyn Francis] – that, in spite of my age, I should offer myself for this task. The way in which the people concerned then worked together in the implementation of my decision gave me the confidence that it was the right decision.[1]

Together with Julian Sleigh, Heinz went again to the seminary in Stuttgart. Their final ordination training, together with Robert Patterson from the United States and Udo Lindenmeyer from Canada, was in Britain (at Woodford House) with Alfred Heidenreich. The four were ordained together in London on May 2, 1965.

After his return to South Africa it became clear that Liselotte and he had drifted apart during Heinz's time in Europe. Liselotte continued working in the day centre while Heinz now had new tasks, without a congregation yet to support him. This led to tensions, and they separated. They had a reconciliation before she died in 1972, Heinz administering the Last Anointing and holding her funeral.

Heinz founded the Community in Cape Town and served it on his own for sixteen years. In 1981 Rachael Clayfield joined him in a fruitful collaboration and it was during her presence that the first permanent home for the Community was found in Ottery, a suburb of Cape Town. Heinz also regularly visited Windhoek in Namibia, where a group of mainly German-speakers invited him to hold Christian Community services.

In 1969 Heinz was in Johannesburg where Neville Adams was about to be inducted by Alfred Heidenreich as the new priest. Just before the great event Heidenreich had a heart attack, and Heinz Maurer carried out the task. Two days later Heidenreich died.

For his seventieth birthday in 1982 Heinz went on a lengthy trip to Europe. He returned to Johannesburg, intending to take a service for an absent colleague, but had a stroke a day after arriving and lost consciousness. He died June 22, 1982.[2]

The Cape

Heinz worked alone in Cape Town until Rachael Clayfield joined him in 1981. In 1985 Neville Adams joined Rachael in Cape Town where the Community had a hall in Ottery. Rachael left in 1992 to work in Chicago and then in London. In 1994 the congregation moved to a new site in Plumstead, where they built a Community

Rachael Shepherd (née Clayfield) in 1991 in London

Cape Town Christian Community centre

Cape Town Christian Community centre

centre including a small chapel that was consecrated at Advent 1996. Richard Goodall, a South African ordained in 1993, has since consolidated the Cape Town congregation.

Julian and Renate Sleigh pioneered a Camphill village for adults with learning disabilities, which was established in 1965 in Dassenberg, north of Cape Town, known today as Camphill Village West Coast. Here, at the centre of the village, in 1969 the first Christian Community church on the continent was built and consecrated. Services are still held in that chapel today.

Julian Sleigh
1927 October 6, Florence, Italy –
2013 October 2, Camphill Village Dassenberg, South Africa

Julian's father was a lecturer at the British Institute in Florence when Julian was born. He began school in Italy, and at the age of ten the family moved to London. When war broke out he was evacuated to Windsor. Already as a schoolboy he showed leadership qualities, being a patrol leader and then troop leader in the Boy Scouts. At the end of the war in 1945 he went to study economics at the London School of Economics, and on completing his studies was called up into the army. He was one of the few from his intake to be chosen for officer training.

On completing his national service Julian took a postgraduate degree in administration. He then got a job as a management trainee at an engineering firm. After two years he sought a change and applied for a job with another engineering firm in Anglesey, Wales. While working there he met Trevor Ravenscroft (later author of *Spear of Destiny*), and through him heard of Rudolf Steiner and anthroposophy.

This led him to visit and then work in Camphill, Scotland for some years. There he experienced the Act of Consecration of Man for the first time. When Julian entered Camphill he made it clear that he was a practising Catholic and attended mass every Sunday. He was given a group of boys to care for, and trained at the Camphill seminar – an evening course. Before long he was also

Julian Sleigh

doing administrative tasks in the central office. Among the young people working in Camphill at that time were Taco Bay, and also Renate, Karl König's daughter.

After Karl König's visit to South Africa in 1957, Renate emigrated to help start Camphill's work there. Julian followed a few months later. They worked together at Hermanus in the Cape. In 1959 they were married by Peter Roth and in the ensuing years they had five children.

By the early 1960s it was becoming clear that a village community for adults with learning disabilities was needed. Around this time Julian asked himself whether he should become a Christian Community priest while remaining totally committed to Camphill – similar to Peter Roth's dual role. When Evelyn Francis came to visit in 1962 he broached the subject with her, and was surprised to hear that Heinz Maurer, too, was thinking of becoming a priest.

And so in late 1963 Julian arrived in Europe with his family.

5. SOUTHERN AFRICA

*The chapel in Camphill Village West Coast,
the first purpose-built chapel in South Africa*

Renate and the children moved to Botton Village while Julian went to Stuttgart. After a year in Germany, Julian, Heinz Maurer and two others completed their final training in Britain and were ordained in London.

Julian (with family) and Heinz immediately returned to South Africa to become the founding priests of The Christian Community there. Initially the main tasks were for Heinz to build the congregation in Cape Town and for Julian to establish a new Camphill village, as well as for both to visit Johannesburg regularly. During Julian's absence, Alpha, a sandy undeveloped farm near Cape Town, had been acquired. In September 1965, just four months after returning from Europe, Julian celebrated the birth of the new initiative for disabled adults, Camphill Village, his base for the rest of his life.

For many years Julian was involved in the telephone counselling service, Lifeline. This work led him to write his book, *Crisis Points*, which has been translated into a dozen languages.

His leadership qualities were again called on when in 1985 he was asked to be lenker of The Christian Community's work in Southern Africa, and initially also of Australia and New Zealand. This involved three trips to Australasia, the first with Michael Tapp and the last with Rosalind Pecover. In 2004 he also visited Manila in the Philippines where he had been invited by a group of anthroposophists who had read his book, *Crisis Points*.

He worked at the Camphill Village in South Africa until his retirement after the age of seventy, and lived there until his death a few days before his 86th birthday.[3]

Johannesburg

In 1936 Kurt and Aenne Schneider, two Christian Community members of Jewish origin, fled from Germany to Johannesburg. Kurt Schneider resolved to continue paying his monthly contribution to the Community, 'Because one day we will have a Christian Community here.'[4] Evelyn Francis had visited Johannesburg on her early trips, and once the Community was established in South Africa, Heinz Maurer and Julian Sleigh visited regularly. The congregation was officially established in 1965 after the founding in Cape Town, but it was only in 1969 that a newly ordained South African priest, Neville Adams, came to work there full time. Kurt Schneider's fund by then had grown so that it largely covered Neville's time of training.

After a year, the congregation bought premises which served both as priest's residence and had a small chapel. Then in 1973 they moved again to the present site in Ferndale, though it did not offer a suitable chapel. However, they built the beautiful Lazarus Church, which was consecrated in 1976. If necessary the church can seat two hundred people, but still feels intimate with only twenty people.

After Heidenreich's death his son Michael, who was working as a priest in Berlin, became deputy lenker for South Africa. He encouraged Neville Adams to hold children's camps and asked Georg

5. SOUTHERN AFRICA

Georg Dreissig, Julian Sleigh, Heinz Maurer, Neville Adams around 1979

The foundation gathering of the congregation in Johannesburg in 1965. In the centre Alfred Heidenreich, Evelyn Francis on the left (turning to her side, above the girl in the white blouse), Heinz Maurer and Julian Sleigh to the left of the pillar Neville Adams fourth to the right of the pillar.

Dreissig to help with them. Georg was an experienced camp leader from Germany who was at the priests' seminary. After ordination he worked in Johannesburg for three years.

From Johannesburg regular visits were made to Durban and Pretoria, as well as occasional visits to the Camphill school in Botswana. However, real development in these places could really only take place if there was a resident priest. Peter van Breda, a South African, came to Johannesburg in 1980. This stimulated new possibilities of growth, and a vibrant Community life unfolded which spanned all ages from 'before birth to beyond death'. Neville left and went to Germany until 1985 when he returned to South Africa, this time to Cape Town. Peter was on his own for some years until Reingard Knausenberger joined him in 1991. Today there are two priests in Johannesburg.

Neville Adams
1939 November 15, Pretoria, South Africa

Neville Adams trained as a pharmacist and became manager of the Weleda Pharmacy in Rosebank, a suburb of Johannesburg. Through this he came into contact with anthroposophy, which opened up a whole new world, and found he was able to reconcile his belief in reincarnation with Christianity. He had many questions, and was told one day that a lady was coming from London who would be able to answer all his questions. Indeed Evelyn Francis did answer many of his questions.

Neville had grown restless in his job, as he felt limited in the way he could help people. He considered studying medicine, but woke one morning with the clear decision to become a priest. He asked to speak to Evelyn, who was surprised to hear this, as she was just about to ask him to consider the priesthood.

By 1965 the congregation in Johannesburg was officially founded, but they had no resident priest. The congregation offered to pay the costs of Neville's training in Germany (from the fund Kurt Schneider

5. SOUTHERN AFRICA

The Lazarus Church in Johannesburg, built in 1975

Inside the Lazarus Church

Neville and Joyce Adams in London in 1968

started) so that he could come back as soon as possible as a priest. Evelyn also held the marriage service for Neville and Joyce before they set off for Germany. He was ordained in 1968 and went to London, joining the priest circle there for six months. The plan was for him to work with Heidenreich, but the latter never really had time to pay much attention to Neville.

Neville and Joyce returned to South Africa to pioneer the work in Johannesburg. In March 1969 Heidenreich arrived in Johannesburg for Neville's induction, but that night suffered a heart attack and was unable to hold the service, which Heinz Maurer conducted. Heidenreich told Neville that, as he could not travel, he would have time to help Neville in his work. But two days later Heidenreich died.

So Neville started his work with a baptism of fire, but it seems to have strengthened his and the congregation's resolve. Neville related that he had never felt as inspired and helped as in those first few years of his work: it was as if Heidenreich from beyond the threshold was keeping his promise.

Within a short time the congregation moved from the suburb of Craighall Park to nearby Blairgowrie, where there was a room

5. SOUTHERN AFRICA

*A South African synod in January 1988 Back: Neville Adams, Richard Goodall, Julian Sleigh
Front: Peter van Breda, Rachael Shepherd (née Clayfield),
Evelyn Francis, Walter Brecker, David Wilmot*

*A South African synod around 2000
Left to right: Neville Adams, Richard Goodall, Reingard Knausenberger,
Ita Bay, Taco Bay, Julian Sleigh, Peter van Breda, David Wilmot*

for a chapel as well as accommodation for Neville and Joyce and their first son. Hopes to buy adjoining land on which to build a chapel came to nought, and so they searched for another site. The house they found in Ferndale (a little further north) was fine for the priest's family but unsuitable for community activities. But the site was large enough to build a church, which they duly did in 1976.

Had it not been for Neville's diligent overseeing of the project the builder (who until then had only erected square buildings) might not quite have managed the construction of the beautiful church with 23 corners.

As well as working in Johannesburg, Neville regularly visited Durban in the province of Natal, and Pretoria (where he also celebrated in Afrikaans), and occasionally German-speaking Windhoek in Namibia. A new activity that Neville brought to South Africa was children's camps and youth work.

Soon after a new South African colleague, Peter van Breda, came to Johannesburg, Neville left alone for Germany for almost three years, and then in 1985 returned to Cape Town where he found a site in Plumstead for a purpose-built Community centre with a small chapel. It was also down to Neville's prompt action that the site for the church and congregation centre in Windhoek was found and could be purchased.

In 1998 Neville separated from Joyce and went to work in Germany in various congregations. He retired in 2007.[5]

Natal

Neville Adams visited Durban from time to time. In 1985 David Wilmot came with his family, and a home was found in Hillcrest where a single garage was converted into a small chapel that could hold a dozen people. David and his wife carried out various enterprises gathering many people around them in the process. As it was not possible to build a church at that residential property, a new rural property was acquired in Shongweni, between Durban and Pietermaritzburg.

In 2005 David was asked to stop work as a priest as some of his actions were deemed incompatible with priestly work. This situation brought Community work to a halt. The resulting sale of the property and healing of this crisis in the congregation took some ten years to resolve.

The congregation now has a new home in Hillcrest with a section converted to a worthy chapel space, and adjacent living quarters for the priest's family. Since 2008 Peter Holman has been working there.

Translating the sacraments into Afrikaans

South Africans of Dutch descent speak Afrikaans, a language that has diverged much more from its Dutch mother language than American English has from British English. Outside the cities it is spoken much more widely than English. Heinz Maurer and Helene

Helene de Villiers (1921–2015) helped translate the rituals into Afrikaans [J C de Villiers]

Chapel on Kiekebusch's farm [Sketch by Eberhard von Koenen]

The church in Windhoek, Namibia

de Villiers (1921–2015) worked on a translation of the rituals with input from Neville Adams and François Maritz. This was then used to celebrate the sacraments in Afrikaans, both in the Cape and in Pretoria (which is predominantly Afrikaans speaking).

Namibia

Heinz Maurer regularly visited Windhoek in Namibia, where a group of mainly German-speakers asked to have services. Namibia was a former German colony so for some time German was an official language there; since independence English has become the official language, though even now German is still widely spoken. Just as some former British colonies retained strong British traditions, so Namibia retained a strong German culture among its mainly cattle-farming settlers.

Activities began on Christoph Kiekebusch's farm about 40 km from Windhoek on Khomas Hochland. There, next to stables built in 1900 for mounted troops, stood a barn, which was converted into a chapel and consecrated by Diether Lauenstein in 1974.

Around 1986, after Neville Adams had undertaken regular visits, a small house was acquired in Windhoek with a room for a chapel, but later this was sold and a larger property was bought. In 1991 Klaus Raschen was sent to Windhoek as resident priest, and his wife Sabine, along with some Community members, also started a Waldorf kindergarten on the property. A church with community rooms was built later. Services are mainly celebrated in German but also in English and Afrikaans.

One of the members, Christine Voigts, started a regular Saturday farmers' market in front of the chapel. This has become an important social event, which also helps the Community financially.

6.
Australia and New Zealand

In Europe or North America we often mention these two countries in one breath as close neighbours. On a map of the world they do seem close, but we must not forget that the Tasman Sea is some 2000 km wide – over three hours' flying time. Nevertheless, their relationship to The Christian Community is closely interlinked.

First visits

Eileen Hersey was the first priest to visit Australia and New Zealand in 1968. Following Heidenreich's cosmopolitan endeavour to make the work of The Christian Community known throughout the English-speaking world, Eileen contacted all the subscribers to the journal offering to visit. Encouraged by the response and invitations, she set off to what she called the Antipodes, visiting North America and Fiji on the way to New Zealand. There she visited Auckland, Hawkes Bay, Christchurch and Wellington, speaking to different groups and holding services as well as christenings. She then repeated this in Australia. When she arrived in Sydney, she found her hostess, Kyra Pohl, had died the day before, and so the first Act of Consecration of Man in Australia was at the same time a memorial service. One of those attending that service was Rosalind Pecover.

Eileen made another trip in 1971. As well as visiting the same places in New Zealand, she also went to Melbourne and Adelaide in Australia. The interest shown led to a foundation group being set up in each country to collect funds. In Australia John Shaw, a lawyer, was

6. AUSTRALIA AND NEW ZEALAND

the driving force behind this, and has remained a firm supporter of the Community ever since. In New Zealand Phyllis Satchell was not only Eileen's 'chauffeur' as she put it; she was one of the key figures in the foundation group.

At the age of 73, Eileen made a third visit in 1974. By this time a student from each country was training at Shalesbrook (however, neither completed their priest's training). The number of people interested in joining The Christian Community in New Zealand and in Australia had grown, and plans began to be made for more concrete steps towards establishing it.

Eileen Hersey was unable to make further visits because of her failing health and there was a gap of five years before Michael Tapp visited in 1979. In 1982 he went again, together with Maarten Udo de Haes, lenker for Holland and a member of the Circle of Seven, and Rosalind Pecover who was then a student at the seminary in Stuttgart. Two years later Michael visited again with Julian Sleigh. This was followed by visits almost every year by different priests.

Eileen Hersey in Johannesburg on her way back from Australia

Michael Tapp
1933 April 1, London – 2014 July 30, Stroud, England

Michael had a penetrating intellect and a capacity to see what was needed in situations. He sacrificed his time and energy selflessly, particularly in the many moves that he undertook. From an early age, he was responsible and mature beyond his years. His devotion to the task of priest and later lenker was never in doubt. While he clearly had aims and ideals, he was very pragmatic in his approach. He looked out for initiative and then whole-heartedly supported it, helping guide it and bring it to fruition.

He embodied something of the Stoic – a quality that many Englishmen of his generation had. He also had something of the puritan – he could see clearly what was needed, and set stringent standards for himself in how to attain the ideal. He was always self-effacing and modest.

In his early years Michael attended a number of schools, including boarding schools. Among these was the Michael Hall School in Forest Row, which he attended for a few years in early childhood. Later he asked to return there, entering in Class 9. He spent Class 12 in Stuttgart, where Michael Heidenreich was a schoolmate. This brought about his first meeting with Alfred Heidenreich, who took the boys out once when he was visiting his son.

While studying history at University College London, Michael discovered the church in Glenilla Road. From the first moment, The Christian Community was a matter of course for him. He became a keen member of Heidenreich's youth group, and attended youth conferences in Keswick. It was also a matter of course for him to become a priest, and Heidenreich fully supported his decision. There is a perhaps apocryphal tale that even then, Dr Heidenreich saw a potential lenker in this young man.

In Stuttgart Michael met Elisabeth Hesse from Denmark, who was also attending the seminary. They were married in 1961 at the church in Glenilla Road two years after Michael was ordained.

6. AUSTRALIA AND NEW ZEALAND

Michael Tapp

He was sent first to work with Oliver Mathews in Stourbridge, from where he also visited Gloucester. The Tapps moved to Bristol in 1962, where they celebrated the service every two weeks, alternating with Gloucester. Michael led the building project of the new church in Stroud, where the family, now with two young children, Veronica and Jonathan, moved in 1968.

In 1972, they moved to Forest Row, where Michael was asked to help with the British priests' training at Shalesbrook. Michael had always been involved in the administration of The Christian Community, and when Oliver Mathews retired in 1974, he was asked to become lenker. This was no easy task, as he was young for this office, and it took time for the older generation of priests to accept him.

Michael continued to run youth camps through the seventies, as it was hard to find other colleagues to take this on. He also became the editor of *The Threshing Floor*, as the *Christian Community Journal* was renamed. In 1979, the family moved to London to obviate the extra journey from Forest Row to London, before any other journey could begin.

In a scrap of a biographical note that Michael wrote, probably at the time he became lenker, he concluded, 'Perhaps as motto: No world traveller – continuous concentration on England (also as seminarist).'[1] But now this motto was to be turned on its head, for in 1979 Michael and Elisabeth visited the Christian Community groups in Australia and New Zealand for three months, travelling via America and returning via South Africa.

Here was a case where he could see initiative that needed a response, and he visited again in 1982 and in 1984. He also saw the need for an experienced priest to be there at the founding in these countries. So he passed on his responsibilities in Britain and in 1988 went to Sydney to found The Christian Community in Australia, staying a few months before he and Elisabeth moved on to New Zealand. From the beginning he was lenker for this new region. The years building up the Community in Australia and New Zealand were happy ones. The directness and spontaneity of the people there helped Michael to overcome his reserve.

He retired in 2001 and he and Elisabeth returned to Stroud in England. In 2011, there was a great community celebration of their golden wedding anniversary. By then it was becoming apparent that Michael was losing full command of his faculties, but he had prepared a speech, which he gave with great aplomb.

After that, his decline continued and eventually he moved into a nursing home suffering mild dementia. It was possible to hold a conversation with him, although he seemed at times to float in and out of focus. Tom Ravetz wrote:

> Some of the cares and concerns from his time as lenker returned to plague him in these years. However, he could reflect on what was happening to him, and something quite new appeared:
> a beatific smile, with a hint of resignation – 'look at silly old me, what I'm getting confused about' – and a deep acknowledgment of the other. He always said a gracious thank you at the end of a visit.[2]

6. AUSTRALIA AND NEW ZEALAND

*Rosalind Pecover with Karl Kaltenbach,
General Secretary of the Anthroposophical Society,
at the founding of The Christian Community in Sydney*

The founding

Finally in 1987 it was decided that the founding of The Christian Community would take place in Australia at Advent 1988 and in New Zealand at Michaelmas 1989. This region probably had one of the longest processes from exploratory visits to founding with a resident priest.

A year before the founding the Sydney group – by now having formed an incorporated trust – bought suitable premises in the suburb of Balmain that could be converted to a chapel and priest's residence. Many people, particularly John Mitchell and his family, put in a lot of work to get the building ready for its new purpose: clearing and planting the old tennis court, and turning the dilapidated clubhouse into a worthy chapel.

Rosalind Pecover, having worked in Frankfurt for five years after her ordination, finally returned to Australia to become the founding priest there. After passing on his responsibilities in Britain to others, Michael Tapp came to work in Australia until the founding in New Zealand.

On Advent Sunday, November 27, 1988, after an extraordinarily powerful dawn thunderstorm, the founding Act of Consecration of Man took place in the new chapel, which was filled to capacity. On the following Sundays similar founding services took place in Adelaide, Canberra and Bowral (between Sydney and Canberra).

In the following year Arie Boogert, an experienced priest from Holland, came as a second priest to Australia. The two priests, based in Sydney, also visited the other congregations, including Perth, some 4000 km away.

In New Zealand, too, the foundation group had acquired a property in the suburbs of Auckland. It had a large room that could accommodate fifty people, and a half-converted double garage as a potential social space, as well as accommodation for the priest.

Kevin Coffey, a New Zealander ordained in 1987 in Germany, returned to work with Michael Tapp, and on Michaelmas Sunday, October 1, 1989, the Auckland Community was founded. From there, Hawkes Bay, Wellington and Christchurch were visited regularly.

In 1991 the congregation in Hawkes Bay managed to buy a suitable house as a centre for the Community's activities.

Rosalind Pecover
1946 November 3, Sydney

Rosalind grew up on a farm and always had a strong relationship to nature: as a young child she saw God in a meadow flower. When she was four or five years old she saw a rainbow, and told her mother that she was going to walk to the end of the rainbow to find the gold. She trained as a teacher in New South Wales and did her in-service training at Inala Rudolf Steiner School for Curative Education in 1967, where she first met anthroposophy. After teaching history of art for a couple of years she travelled through Asia to Europe to see some the art at first hand. Her travels then took her from Britain to Toronto, Canada, where she worked for two years.

In Australia, Rosalind had attended the first Act of Consecration of Man in 1968, as it was also the memorial service of Kyra Pohl, the director of Inala School. But it was in Toronto through Werner Grimm that she consciously got to know The Christian Community in 1973. Here she felt for the first time that she had found the gold at the end of the rainbow.

Her return journey to Australia took her through South America, working for a time in Peru, and through South Africa where she met Neville Adams in Johannesburg. On the ship from Cape Town to Sydney at end of 1974 her decision to train for the priesthood and bring the sacraments to Australia ripened. At this stage she did not know there was already a group in Sydney preparing for founding The Christian Community in Australia. On finding this group, and discussing her intentions with John Shaw, he replied, 'If you want to do this, you have my support.' This marked the beginning of a long collaboration between Rosalind Pecover and John Shaw, working towards the founding.

She started her training in 1976 at Shalesbrook and continued in Stuttgart. One of her breaks for practical congregational work was in Australia preparing for the founding. She was ordained in 1983 and worked in Frankfurt for some years before returning to Australia with Michael Tapp as a founding priest in Sydney in 1988.

Rosalind was strong-willed and worked tirelessly in building up the Community in Sydney, often at the cost of her health. She was the driving force behind the purchase of the factory building adjoining the site of the Community, and the building of a centre there. It was perhaps her declining health that led her to be dazzled by the unrealistic promises of a persuasive financial investor, which brought about the massive loss on the half-built property in 2008. She retired after this disaster.[3]

PIONEERS OF RELIGIOUS RENEWAL

Cheryl and Michael Nekvapil with John Shaw

The ordination of Cheryl Nekvapil at Canberra 2002
Left to right: Michael Tapp, Elke Baublies, Lisa Devine, Ita Bay, Erin Ketel, Taco Bay, Martin Samson, Cheryl Nekvapil, Hartmut Borries, Rosalind Pecover

6. AUSTRALIA AND NEW ZEALAND

New priests

In 1992 Hartmut Borries from Germany and Martin Samson, who was born in South Africa, came to work in Australia.

Hartmut went to Melbourne in 1996. In about 2004 what had been an old wooden church was rebuilt in a style more appropriate to the renewed sacraments. It is the nearest to a purpose-built Christian Community chapel in Australia. After Michael Tapp retired and returned to Britain in 2001, Hartmut became lenker for a time. Later he moved to New Zealand and now works in Auckland.

Martin was sent to Adelaide in 1995. There an old sandstone stable was renovated as a chapel in 1997, the first consecrated chapel in Australia. Martin has run excursions into the Australian outback to explore the connection between Aboriginal Australia and the southern stars, and after many years of running courses and lecturing wrote his book, *Festivals in the Southern Hemisphere.*

In 2001 Lisa Devine was ordained, and then worked in Melbourne. In the following year Cheryl Nekvapil was ordained in Canberra where she was to work. It was the first ordination in the southern hemisphere. In 2015 she moved to Melbourne and took on the responsibilities of lenker of Australia and New Zealand.

Sydney's disaster

In 1997 the factory building in a corner of the Community's site in Balmain was bought, as it offered the possibility of a larger chapel. The Community had slightly less than half the money in hand, and took a mortgage for the balance. To finance the mortgage payment they took a further mortgage of more than double that amount and invested it with a hedge-fund manager. In 2004 it was decided to renovate the factory building to actually use as a chapel, and to build a Community centre. There was some money in hand to start this work but again a mortgage was taken and put into a hedge fund.

Members, friends and the congregation in Perth made further loans and also invested in the same hedge fund. The conversion and new building was started.

Then came the financial crash of 2008 and of course the hedge fund collapsed – it was probably a Ponzi scheme. No clear written agreements had been made and the situation was unclear. Rosalind Pecover's health had deteriorated, and she was given leave of absence; a new priest, Sune Nielsen, who had arrived in 2007 also left the work. The Sydney congregation was left without a resident priest, and many left, having lost all their personal savings. On the site was the shell of a new building and a partly converted chapel. As soon as payments stopped, so did the builder.

During this critical time Cheryl Nekvapil from Canberra and Martin Samson from Adelaide visited regularly. Eventually a core of members, notably John Shaw who had been there from the beginning, awoke to the reality of the huge loss of some three million Australian dollars. The whole site was sold, and an old Methodist chapel in Balmain was bought and converted into a more modest chapel and community rooms.

In this land of drought and fire, the Sydney Community experienced a kind of baptism by fire, which affected not only this congregation but the others in Australia.

The present situation

In Australia there are resident priests in Sydney, Canberra, Melbourne and Adelaide; Perth in Western Australia and Queensland are visited. In New Zealand it has not been easy to sustain the work, although all four centres from 1989 are still there today. Only Auckland has resident priests. The two active and two retired priests visit Hawkes Bay, Wellington and Christchurch.

In a part of the world where there is no great deference to authority, members are very active and carry a lot of responsibility and initiative, but congregations are relatively small and almost all the priests have part-time additional jobs to survive financially.

There is a real effort to work together despite the tremendous distances separating the congregations.

The Philippines

Gisela Wielki from America had held talks about The Christian Community for groups of interested people while she was on vacation in the Philippines, and later Julian Sleigh gave a workshop there in 2004 about his book *Crisis Points*. Soon afterwards a request came for a confirmation service. Neville Adams went there in 2005 and again in 2006 to hold this service. Since then priests have occasionally visited the Philippines.

7.
Conclusion

Over recent decades The Christian Community has spread to Japan and to southern and eastern Europe – Italy, Spain, Russia, Ukraine, Hungary, Romania and Georgia. In the countries where it has been established for longer, growth has slowed. Like a living organism, growth is not constant but goes in spurts, and it could be said that the Community has had a very visible burst of growth and flowering (in its initial phase and again in the 1950s and 1960s), and is now in a more inwardly focused stage, where fruits are ripening for future seeds. Perhaps it helps to remember that Christianity itself took time to spread and grow and find its way in the world, so we should not be surprised that The Christian Community is also taking time to find its way in today's world, where many people no longer have a clear yearning for outward forms of religion.

Nevertheless, despite hardships and setbacks, many people have persevered to nurture this movement and to bring a deep reverence to the sacraments, as they are worthily celebrated in a form that speaks to hearts and minds today.

Having read of some of the failures and crises, as well as the great initiatives and achievements, and seen how The Christian Community is evolving and developing, we can think of Wilhelm Hochweber's words, after his foray to the United States of America in 1929:

> I think the world needs us; needs our best and our mistakes –
> if only they are always new mistakes, and not the old ones which have already been made.[1]

Appendix

The 48 founding priests (in order or ordination)

There were 45 priests ordained in Dornach in September 1922. Three more, ordained in the months afterwards, are also regarded as founding priests, as they were intimately involved in the events leading to the founding. Ordinations are carried out in order of age. At this first ordination oberlenkers and lenkers were ordained before the others. The following brief biographical notes are distilled from Gädeke, *Die Gründer*.

1. Friedrich Rittelmeyer
1872 October 5, Dillingen, Bavaria – 1938 March 23, Hamburg
See p. 18ff.

Ordained on September 16, 1922 by Friedrich Rittelmeyer

2. Emil Bock
1895 May 19, Barmen (now Wuppertal) – 1959 December 6, Stuttgart
See p. 27ff.

3. Johannes Werner Klein
1898 June 24, Düsseldorf – 1984 March 9, Hamburg

Aged seventeen Klein enlisted voluntarily, serving first in Russia, then in France where he became an officer. By 1918 he saw clearly that Germany would lose the war, and lost his will to live. However, on leave in the Harz mountains, he saw a young woman from a distance, who renewed his will to live. Though he had not spoken a word to her, he wrote to her from the front but found she was engaged.

His life was turbulent, alternately showing an enthusiastic, charismatic and gifted side in student circles, and then sinking into lonely depression. Through his sister, he heard of anthroposophy and decided to study theology at Marburg where he met Martin Borchart. In February 1920 he went to Dornach, and in a conversation with Steiner, asked about a third church, beyond Catholic and Protestant. Steiner replied, 'the forms can be found', but Klein misunderstood this to mean that he had to create the forms, so he set out a plan of lengthy theological studies to accomplish this. In 1921 he met Getrud Spörri (she had also asked Steiner about religious renewal) who told him Steiner was willing to give a theological course. His error dawned on him. With Spörri he gathered together eighteen students for the June Course in Stuttgart.

When Christian Geyer withdrew before the founding, Klein became one of the oberlenkers, together with Rittelmeyer and Bock. He started work in Hamburg. In 1924 he asked Steiner for a course on the Apocalypse, the last course Steiner gave to the priests before his death.

In a conversation Steiner confirmed that Klein's relationship to the young woman he had seen in the mountains was an old connection of destiny, which had also led to his seeking the priesthood. Although she was married and had a daughter, Klein called Emma Krille 'Petra', his rock, and had a lifelong obsession with her. After this conversation with Steiner, he took up contact with her again. His writings show that he projected much of his own feelings onto her, and became dependent on these delusions – everything was subordinated to 'Petra'.

In 1929 he resigned from the Anthroposophical Society and stepped out of the priesthood – the first apostate. Later he became a member of the Nazi Party, and during the Second World War he married Emma Krille.

Bock visited him after the war but was disappointed. A few months after Klein's death in 1984 Emma took her life.

Despite being one of the prime movers in the beginnings of The Christian Community, in Klein we see a tragic destiny of one who could not ground his life out of a truly free individual striving.

4. Gertrud Spörri
1894 December 8, Bärenswil, Zurich – 1968 July 16, Rüti, Zurich

Spörri had to leave school early when her father's textile factory had financial problems and she became his secretary. She grew up in Swiss Calvinist tradition and was always searching. Once, listening to a sermon about Calvin, she had a vision of a priest in vestments at the altar, and was shocked to realise this was herself. This eventually led her to study theology in 1920 in Basle, from where she could regularly visit Dornach (she had heard of anthroposophy in 1913).

In a conversation about religion with Steiner in May 1920 he offered to hold a course for a group of theologians, and mentioned that two students from Marburg had asked him similar questions. (Spörri had in fact briefly met J.W. Klein and Borchart at the time of their Dornach visit.) During the student course in September 1920 they met properly, also with Rudolf Meyer, and soon began contacting potential students for a theology course. Klein had drafted a request to Steiner, but when Spörri went to Berlin and showed it to Bock, he was witheringly critical of its obsequious tone. Only in May 1921 at the student course in Stuttgart did Husemann succeed in drafting a request to Steiner that everyone was happy with, which led to the first theological course in June 1921. After this Spörri returned to Switzerland to raise finances (German hyperinflation was beginning) and make practical arrangements for the Autumn Course (accommodation, visa applications).

At the founding she was made a titular (or honorary) oberlenker and worked in Stuttgart with Rittelmeyer, Bock and Beckh. In 1933 sadly there was a rift. Two priests, Hermann and Helmut Weidelehner (brothers), broke their priestly vow never to alter the ritual texts by changing them, out of what they claimed to be 'a higher revelation'. Spörri supported them in this change. This led to all three (as well as Jutta Frentzel) leaving The Christian Community in 1933. Spörri eventually returned to Switzerland, worked for the Red Cross and later in a tuberculosis sanatorium. Inwardly she distanced herself from the Community, even saying to someone in the 1950s that she had no need for anthroposophy.

5. Johannes Perthel
1888 September 6, Leukersdorf, Chemnitz – 1944 July 20, Friedrichshafen

Since childhood Perthel was a loner, an outsider. Born into a strict Lutheran minister's family, he studied liberal theology in Marburg. He became a minister and in 1915 married Mechthild Grohmann (sister of the Goethean botanist). He was called up for the last eighteen months of the war, serving as army chaplain. His early years in the newly formed congregation of a mining village in Saxony were difficult: there was no church, meeting room or even rectory. Through someone in the youth movement he heard of anthroposophy and, through reading books, he slowly began to make sense of it. Meyer visited and invited him to the Autumn Course, and during the foundation course Steiner suggested him as lenker. He went on to found the Leipzig congregation with Frieling, then was in Breslau from 1926 until the *Verbot*. In 1944, while going to visit Marta Heimeran in the south of Germany, he was killed in an air raid on Friedrichshafen station.

6. Friedrich Doldinger
1897 December 2, Radolfzell, Lake Constance – 1973 September 2, Freiburg

None of the founding priests worked in one congregation for as long as Doldinger, for after the founding he went to Freiburg and worked there until he died. Born into a Catholic family, he went to secondary school in Freiburg when his father, a postmaster, was transferred there. He was artistic and musical, and often top of the class, but suffered from poor health throughout his life (and was later excused from military service). Aged sixteen a friend of the family took him to a lecture by Steiner. By the time he was studying music and literature in Freiburg, he was writing and lecturing on anthroposophical subjects. Tom Kändler invited him to the Autumn Course. From the beginning he was lenker for Baden and Switzerland and travelled a lot throughout his region. He did not like sitting in meetings and often did not turn up for lenker sessions. It was not easy for any colleague to work with him in Freiburg. He was eccentric, with a sense of humour, and always keen on improvisation and artistic activities; holding a sermon on the Apocalypse he pulled out a trumpet and blew on it to illustrate the heralding of the event. Once at a confirmation his entire sermon to the young people consisted of, 'You can get through life with relatively few sins. Yea, so be it.'

7. Alfred Heidenreich
1898 January 17, Regensburg – 1969 March 11, Johannesburg
See p. 41ff.

8. Rudolf von Koschützki
1866 April 8, Tarnowitz, Kattowitz, Silesia (now Tarnowskie Góry, Katowice, Poland) – 1954 March 16, Stuttgart

At 56, Koschützki was the oldest of the founders, with a great mane of white hair, giving him the nickname of Weisser Hengst (White Stallion). He was one of the few without a theological background. His family had been landowners in Silesia for centuries, but during his agricultural apprenticeship at another estate he met Titania who became his wife. In 1891, before marrying her, he was in a train accident, becoming trapped in the wreckage, and eventually freed as the only survivor from that carriage. He suffered from recurring bouts of weakness that put an end to his plans of running agricultural estates, so he turned to writing. (His textbook on agriculture ran through many editions). As editor of a paper for soldiers at the front, he heard Rittelmeyer preach in 1916, and through him later met Steiner. Koschützki felt 'This is either complete madness or the greatest thing since two thousand years.'[1] In Stuttgart in 1921 he stumbled across the gathering of young theologians, which meant nothing to him, but Emil Bock persuaded him to stay. He founded the congregation in Breslau with Rudolf Meyer and Kurt von Wistinghausen, and was present when Steiner gave the Agricultural Course in nearby Koberwitz. Later he worked in Berlin, after the war in Bremen and then in Stuttgart. A few months before his death he made a deep impression at a large youth conference in 1953, where he told of Steiner and the founding steps of The Christian Community.

9. *August Pauli*
1869 July 31, Willanzheim, Würzburg, Bavaria – 1959 January 6, Munich

Born as the second of five children of a Lutheran minister, Pauli studied theology at Erlangen and Tübingen. He worked with Christian Geyer and later in Catholic south Bavaria. He became disillusioned with traditional social forms of the church, and resigned in 1908. He married, and after ten years rejoined the church, working in Thuringia. In 1922, when he heard of the founding of a new religious movement, he broke with the church once more. After the founding he was sent to Munich with Gerhard Klein, who was soon replaced by Hermann Heisler. Both were individualistic fighters: Heisler a fiery speaker; Pauli quieter, with well thought-through reasoning. In 1933 Pauli tried to mediate with Spörri and the Weidelehner brothers before they left the Community. After the war, he started work again in Munich, where he remained until he died at almost ninety.

10. *Hermann Beckh*
1875 May 4, Nürnberg – 1937 March 1, Stuttgart

Born into a well-to-do family, Beckh felt school to be an imposition on his freedom to play and dream. However, he was brilliant, being able to repeat pages of prose after a single reading. Languages came easily to him (he learned fourteen in his lifetime). He studied law in Munich and became a magistrate. One of his first cases involved the theft of firewood by a poor couple with a young child. If he imprisoned the couple, the child would be left uncared for, so he fined them instead. They obviously had no money to pay, so Beckh paid the fine himself and resigned from the legal profession.

He then studied ancient languages (Sanskrit, Tibetan, Hindi, Persian, Egyptian) in Kiel and Berlin. He met Rittelmeyer and Steiner in 1911 and soon became a member of the Anthroposophical Society. He wrote on Buddhism, Indology and the development of language. During the First

Hermann Beckh

World War he was drafted into military service but very soon was transferred to clerical duties, evaluating economic reviews in Scandinavian papers (for which he had to learn Scandinavian languages). After the war he resumed university lecturing and was soon made 'extraordinary professor'. However, at the end of 1921 he resigned from academic life.

In March 1922 he heard of the preparatory meeting of the priests-to-be with Rittelmeyer. He simply turned up there, announcing, 'Now I'm here, I'm part of this. Even if you don't want me, you won't get rid of me.' After ordination he worked in Stuttgart, mainly lecturing and teaching at the seminary. He was loving and loveable, and the personification of the forgetful professor.

11. Heinrich Rittelmeyer
1879 June 20, Schweinfurt, Bavaria – 1960 January 19, Wiesbaden

Friedrich Rittelmeyer's younger brother knew from the age of thirteen that he was going to be a minister. He studied theology at Erlangen, Berlin and Munich, and then taught at a Lutheran school in Godesberg, where he met Änne Kottemann whom he married in 1908. His brother told him of Steiner, but it was only some years later that he took an interest, and in 1917 heard Steiner lecture. At 43 he was one of the older priests to be ordained in 1922. Initially he worked in Mannheim and Heidelberg, then Herford and Bielefeld. In 1935 he was sent to Mainz and Wiesbaden where he worked for the rest of his life. He was a quiet, modest man who prayed intensely for his congregation and for those who had died.

12. Fritz Blattmann
1882 October 18, Barr, Alsace (now France)
– 1969 October 11, Beddelhausen, Siegen-Wittgenstein

Born in newly conquered Alsace (his father was a civil servant posted there), Fritz was a brilliant child who studied theology at Tübingen on a scholarship. As a minister he served in seaman's missions in Marseille and Genoa and once worked incognito as a coalman on a steamer to New York. In 1914 he left the church, and was called up for the duration of the war. In 1916 he became engaged and through his fiancée heard of anthroposophy. He built up a large group of anthroposophists, including many workers, with Alfred Meebold in Heidenheim, Germany. Through Hermann Heisler he became part of the founding circle, and subsequently worked in Heidenheim, where most of the anthroposophists came to The Christian Community. This led to Steiner's remarks about distinguishing the Anthroposophical Society from The Christian Community, distinguishing a striving for knowledge and for religion. After a year he was sent to Göppingen, and in 1931 to Mannheim, where he finally married. After seven years he went to Darmstadt where he worked (interrupted by the *Verbot*) until he retired in 1963 aged 81.

13. Hermann Fackler
1886 April 10, Lörrach, Baden Württemberg – 1978 July 19, Stuttgart

Fackler was born in Lörrach with a Protestant father and Catholic mother who died in childbirth. On visits to Catholic relatives the mass made a deep impression on him. He studied theology, became a trainee minister, and married. Dissatisfied with intellectual theology, he became interested in the mystical ideas of Arthur Drews (author of *The Christ Myth*). While working as a minister in Rheinfelden (south-west Germany) a blind parishioner asked Fackler to take him to Dornach to see the 'crazy building' of Steiner. Fackler obliged and their visit made a deep impression on him, and led to several more visits and reading Steiner's book. Rudolf Meyer invited him to the Autumn Course. He worked in Konstanz, Berlin, Nürnberg, Göppingen and from 1936 in Reutlingen.

Ordained on September 16, 1922 by Emil Bock

14. Wilhelm Ruhtenberg
1888 January 17, Riga, Russian Empire (now Latvia)
– 1954 August 31, Bensberg, Cologne

Born in Riga (then part of the Russian Empire) to a German merchant family, Ruhtenberg studied theology before working as a teacher, and later a minister. He married, had two daughters, and read Steiner as part of his personal philosophy studies. In 1919 he fled Latvia's civil war to Stuttgart and became a Waldorf teacher there, as well as teaching religion. Steiner had given him the baptism and marriage ritual text before The Christian Community was founded. He took part in all Steiner's courses and was ordained, but remained a teacher in Stuttgart until 1930. He worked as a priest in Rostock, Leipzig and Chemnitz until the *Verbot*. He did not take up work in the Community after the war but went into education for special needs.

15. Claus von der Decken
1888 October 5, Neuhaus/Elbe, Lower Saxony – 1977 August 24, Kassel

Claus von der Decken was from a land-owning family, studied art in Munich and Paris and became a portrait painter of the aristocracy, something he continued from time to time to supplement his income after becoming a priest. While serving in the military, he married (the even more aristocratic) Cécile von Hodenburg in 1916, and they had seven children. He had met Steiner in Düsseldorf, but took some years to make a firm connection with the group. Rudolf Meyer invited him to the Autumn Course. He worked in Hanover with Otto Becher, where Cécile died in 1928. From 1931 to the end of his life Decken then worked in Kassel, remarrying in 1932.

16. Wilhelm Salewski
1889 September 20, Chemnitz
– 1950 February 1, Unterlengenhardt, Pforzheim

Salewski was the oldest of twelve children, came top of his class and studied philosophy in Greifswald, Marburg, Tübingen and Berlin. He served in the First World War and met anthroposophy (it is not known exactly how). His doctoral thesis was not accepted as it contained too much anthroposophy. He lectured on the Steiner's threefold social order. From the Autumn

Course onwards he was part of the founding group. He started work in Düsseldorf, soon after went to Karlsruhe, then Stettin (now Szczecin in Poland) until the *Verbot*. After the war he worked in Bayreuth.

17. *Otto Becher*
1891 January 26, Holzminden, Göttingen – 1954 July 19, Pforzheim

Becher was a brilliant student who received a grant to study in Leipzig and Göttingen. He met Rudolf Meyer in 1916 and through him found anthroposophy. Despite studying theology he went on to become a private teacher. He was one of the eighteen who took part in the June Course. After working briefly in Hanover and Görlitz, in 1924 he came to Pforzheim where he worked for the rest of his life. He was a quiet, unassuming and modest person, but well known and respected in the town.

18. *Kurt Philippi*
1892 October 16, Munich – 1955 March 19, Nürnberg

Born in Munich, Philippi went to school in Berlin. He studied theology (interrupted by wartime military service) but did not become a minister, training instead in lecturing and public speaking. He met Rittelmeyer and Bock, and after short spells elsewhere, he worked in Nürnberg. He married, and was called up at the end of war, but immediately after the war returned to his congregation in Nürnberg where he worked to the end of his life.

19. *Heinrich Ogilvie*
1893 July 18, Schleusingen, Suhl, Thuringia
– 1988 February 15, Zeist, Netherlands

Ogilvie's mother died when he was twelve, leading to his resolve to become a minister. He studied theology, was called up, wounded and graduated during convalescence. However, he wanted to work socially. While running a farm he read half of Steiner's *Knowledge of Higher Worlds*, but decided it was 'not for me'. Husemann visited and invited him to the Autumn Course, but despite his wife's urging, he again decided it was 'not for me'. He attended a lecture by Gitzke on religious renewal, but once more decided it was 'not for me'. However, he was sufficiently intrigued to go to Breitbrunn and only then became part of the founding group. At first he worked in Düsseldorf then, following Rittelmeyer and Bock's visit to The Hague in 1925, Ogilvie moved there in January 1926. He held the first Act of Consecration in Dutch in June 1926. He founded congregations

Heinrich Ogilvie

in The Hague, Rotterdam and Amsterdam, and a church was built in The Hague in 1935. In 1938 he became lenker of north-west Germany and the Netherlands. After the Nazi invasion in 1940 The Christian Community was restricted but not forbidden. An order banning Ogilvie from working was issued, but the senior policeman of the same name (and very distantly related), who was to deliver and enforce it, kept reshuffling it to the bottom of his pile of paperwork. After the war Ogilvie worked in Zeist, where he also made a translation of the New Testament into Dutch.

20. *Martin Borchart*
1894 June 3, Berlin – 1971 December 19, Stuttgart

Borchart's father was a headmaster in Berlin. During the First World War he was injured and subsequently volunteered for the air force (during training he flew to his fiancée's village, landing in a nearby field). He married in 1918; his wife was an anthroposophist. He studied in Marburg where he started an anthroposophical group, which Johannes Werner Klein joined. In 1920 he went on a trip to Dornach to hear Steiner speak. He was part of the founding group from the June Course onwards. After briefly working in Dresden and Bayreuth he came to Stuttgart in 1925, where he worked for the rest of his life. He became lenker for Württemberg in 1938. He was a quiet, modest person.

21. Hermann Groh
1894 June 11, Berlin
– 1957 December 14, Jever, Wilhelmshaven, Lower Saxony

At school Groh was very sporty but also interested in philosophy and languages. As a prisoner of war in Russia from 1915 to 1921 he read Steiner's *Knowledge of Higher Worlds*. On his return he met the Tübingen students and took part in the Autumn Course. He worked in Essen where there were no anthroposophical activities. He married Lili (Gerhard Klein's sister) in 1924 in Dornach, with Heidenreich holding the service, and Heimeran and Husemann as witnesses. In 1928 he visited America, but little more is known of this. In 1929 he worked in Vienna, and from 1935 in Dresden. During the Second World War he served as a Russian, French and English interpreter for prisoners of war. After the collapse of the Nazis he gathered a congregation and began celebrating in Berlin. For unknown reasons he stopped work as a priest in 1947 and moved to East Frisia, where he died ten years later.

22. Wolfgang Schickler
1894 July 11, Stuttgart – 1960 September 14, Heidenheim

As an officer during the First World War Schickler read Steiner's *Esoteric Science* in 1917. He married in 1919, campaigned for Steiner's threefold social order, and had to prepare a transcript of the June Course for print. As a result he became part of the founding group. He worked in Heidenheim for the rest of his life. His wife died in 1939 at the birth of their sixth child. He remarried in 1953. He could not resist becoming politically active, and so was asked to stop working as a priest in 1958.

23 Marta Heimeran
1895 October 2, Nürnberg – 1965 May 2, Arlesheim, Switzerland.
See p. 50ff.

24 Adolf Müller
1895 November 4, Doberlug-Kirchhain, Brandenburg
– 1967 January 13, Berlin

A quiet, modest man, Müller had the appearance of a 'lost angel'. Very little is known of his early life – whether he served in the First World War or even how he met anthroposophy (probably through Gitzke who was at school and studied with him). He studied theology in Berlin and became a minister. After the founding he worked in Berlin. During the *Verbot* he continued to celebrate regularly and visited congregations across the increasingly destroyed city. He knew everyone, their addresses and phone numbers by heart. After the war he lived in a derelict house in the centre of Berlin which, after the erection of the wall in 1961, was in the east, cutting him off from the western congregation.

25. Richard Gitzke
1896 May 8, Rendsburg, Schleswig Holstein – 1989 June 1, Murrhardt, Baden Württemberg

At the age of ten, during a boring, unsatisfying sermon, he heard an inner voice saying, 'Be quiet, Richard. When you are older there'll be a new reformation, and you'll be part of it.' After serving in the war he studied theology in Berlin. He was given Steiner's *Esoteric Science,* soon became a member of the Anthroposophical Society, and met Bock and Rittelmeyer. He attended the June Course. He worked first in Kassel, then in Thuringia where he married. In 1939 he was sent to Wuppertal, where in 1956 a church was built. In 1957 he was sent to Siegen, and in 1966 to Bayreuth until his retirement.

Ordained on September 17, 1922
by Johannes Werner Klein

26. Carl Stegmann
1897 March 15, Kiel, Schleswig Holstein – 1996 February 16, Öschelbronn.
See p. 62ff.

27. Erwin Lang
1897 May 11, Neuhausen, Schaffhausen, Switzerland – 1985 April 11, Schopfheim, Baden Württemberg

Born at his parents' hotel at the Rhine Falls, Lang was injured in the First World War and experienced a life panorama. While recuperating in Kiel he read a book by Steiner which made sense of his near death experience. Through Violetta Pinkert, leader of the Anthroposophical Society in Kiel, he got to know Rudolf Meyer. At Breitbrunn he had severe doubts about his suitability for becoming a priest as he had no academic background, made worse by having to give a talk while the eminent anthroposophist Michael Bauer was present. The latter said to him, 'Well done,' and this gave him the confidence to continue. Initially he worked in Bremen for five years, then briefly in Zurich before coming to Karlsruhe for fifty years.

28. Eberhard Kurras
1897 June 28, Berlin – 1981 August 22, Engelberg, Baden Württemberg

A delicate boy, Kurras was excused from sport, singing and religion at school (later colleagues called him Little Alabaster Man). Aged seventeen he found Rittelmeyer's book on ministry, and wrote to him (Rittelmeyer kept his letter). He studied theology in Berlin and saw Rittelmeyer regularly. He heard Steiner lecturing and was part of the founding group from the beginning. He founded congregations in Naumburg, Jena and Weimar before working in Nürnberg from 1934. He was married, and had two sons. He became lenker of Bavaria in 1962 and oberlenker in 1967, though he never fully carried out this office owing to his health.

29. Arnold Goebel
1897 September 1, Halle – 1972 April 25, Stuttgart

Arnold Goebel was the eleventh child of a Lutheran minister. Called up in 1916 and wounded on the Western Front, he took a whole year to regain health. He spent several years studying engineering, mathematics and theology. He was at the student course in Stuttgart in 1921, and met Husemann who invited him to the Autumn Course. From then on he was fully active in the founding group. He worked in Erfurt, Ulm and Frankfurt and built up children's work and religion lessons (for which he was nicknamed Kinder-Goebel). When the Waldorf schools were closed in 1938, Goebel gave religion lessons to huge children's groups. After the war this led to Christian Community religion lessons being given in Waldorf schools in Germany. In 1949 he became lenker for Switzerland and in 1966 oberlenker, but was never fully able to carry out this office due to ill health.

30. Otto Franke
1897 December 27, Berlin – 1956 June 17, Wetzlar, Hesse

Franke joined the air force in the First World War and briefly saw action before the end of the war. He studied theology in Berlin, met Gitzke and Bock, and was part of the founding group from the June Course (partly walking to Stuttgart from Berlin). He worked in Berlin, Rostock, Eisenach and Jena before coming to Marburg in 1940, where he worked to the end of his life. He married in 1934. He was a brilliant academic who matured into a warm, enthusiastic speaker.

31. Walter Gradenwitz
1898 December 5, Wiesbaden – 1960 December 28, Rotterdam

Gradenwitz began studying science and architecture, but changed to theology. He heard of anthroposophy through Hermann Beckh in Berlin and Hermann Heisler in Tübingen. He was part of the founding group from the beginning. He worked in Pforzheim for five years and then founded a congregation in Düsseldorf that had suffered from three previous unsuccessful attempts. Being part Jewish he was sent to Holland in 1935 while his family (with five children) initially stayed in Germany. After learning Dutch, he worked in Rotterdam until the 1940 Nazi invasion when as a Jew he was forbidden from working. After the war he worked in Zeist.

32. Joachim Sydow
1899 July 20, Prenzlau, Brandenburg – 1949 May 4, Everloh, Hanover

Joachim Sydow was born into a Lutheran minister's family in Brandenburg. After injuries in the First World War he studied theology in Berlin, Tübingen and Rostock. Through the Wandervogel movement he met others who were looking for a renewal of religion. In Rostock he played the flute and did puppet shows for children, the newspapers calling him the Pied Piper of Rostock. Husemann found him and invited him to the Autumn Course. After the founding he worked in Rostock, then in Hanover. He married and had two daughters. Called up in 1942, he was not arrested at the time of the *Verbot*. However, he soon developed a progressively deteriorating illness that led to his early death.

33. Rudolf Koehler
1899 December 12, Tetschen, Bohemia (now Děčin, Czech Republic) – 1992 June 19, East Grinstead, UK. See p. 60ff.

Ordained on September 17, 1922 by Friedrich Rittelmeyer

34. Ludwig Köhler
1900 January 4, Greiz, Vogtland, Thuringia – 1985 March 20, Berlin

While a student Köhler always wore a suit and bow tie, and was not part of the Wandervogel. After studying science in Halle, he switched to theology in Leipzig. Twice he was given Steiner's *Theosophy* to read, but put it aside. Then he was given *Christianity as Mystical Fact* and read it immediately.

He went to Dornach for a student course and then continued studying in Tübingen. He was in the founding group from the beginning. He started work in Chemnitz, and married in 1925, then worked in Danzig before coming to Berlin in 1935. In 1938 he was made lenker for northern Germany. At the *Verbot* he was imprisoned with Eduard Lenz, Adolf Müller and some Waldorf teachers. After the war he was lenker for East Germany, but when the wall was built in 1961 he was unable to cross. He worked in West Berlin until the end of his life.

35. Waldemaar Mickisch
1900 January 11, Mansfeld, Saxony Anhalt
– 1944 July 2 (missing in action), Vilnius, Lithuania

Mickisch was at boarding school near Naumburg with Husemann, then studied in Tübingen and Jena. Through Husemann he heard of the new movement and joined it. He worked first in Berlin where he married, then in Dortmund and Essen. He was called up in 1939, and was reported missing in action in 1944. He was quiet, and did not lecture or write (his memorandum declaring his commitment to the new movement consisted of 4½ lines); his strength was pastoral work.

36. Gottfried Husemann
1900 April 18, Lübbecke, North Rhine-Westphalia
– 1972 May 19, Arlesheim, Switzerland

Both Gottfried's older half-brother Friedrich and his younger brother Gisbert became well known anthroposophical physicians. He studied theology in Halle. Friedrich gave him books by Steiner and took him to Dornach. In Stuttgart during the student course in 1921 Spörri gathered theological students and Husemann formulated their letter to Steiner that led to the June Course. He worked in Cologne for nine years – a difficult time, also for his health. In 1929 he became lenker and in 1933, on Spörri's leaving the movement, became oberlenker and seminary leader. He was a fiery character, and others often had difficulties working with him.

37. Jutta Frentzel
1901 March 3, Berlin – 1999 July 23, Augsburg

Frentzel studied theology in Berlin. She heard Steiner speak at a public lecture in Freiburg in 1920 on her way to Tübingen, where she came into contact with Tom Kändler and others. The youngest of the three women founders, Frentzel almost went to the June Course, but despite Bock's encouragement did not. However, by autumn she was fully behind the founding. She had unsuccessful beginnings in Ravensburg and in Erlangen, and after suffering from a lengthy bout of pneumonia, worked with Joachim Sydow in Rostock. After Spörri left the work, Frentzel, too, in 1934, turned her back on The Christian Community. She married, had four children, and lived in Berlin then later in Stuttgart.

38. Rudolf Frieling
1901 March 23, Leipzig – 1986 January 7, Stuttgart.
See p. 56ff.

39. Thomas Kändler
1901 April 10, Eibenstock, Erzgebirge, Saxony – 1957 February 8, Hamburg

Michael Bauer was a family friend. When Tom Kändler was ten Steiner also stayed with the family and gave Tom the evening prayer 'From my head to my feet'. Tom wanted to be a minister, but also felt the need for sacramental ritual, so he studied both Catholic and Protestant theology at Greiz and Tübingen. A clear thinker and good speaker, he was always immaculately dressed and even as a student had a neat and tidy room. He was part of the founding group from the very beginning, and after ordination until his death worked in Hamburg. His son Peter also became a priest who worked in England for a time.

40. Kurt von Wistinghausen
1901 May 13, Reval, Russian Empire (now Tallinn, Estonia) – 1986 March 9, Filderstadt, Stuttgart

Born into a German surgeon's family, Wistinghausen almost died at age fourteen from a burst appendix. In the Russian Revolution the family's property was confiscated and they fled to Berlin. He read German studies and art history in Tübingen where he met Heimeran, Kändler, Sydow and others. As a non-theologian he was not at the June or Autumn Courses. Only in 1922 did Heidenreich ask him to join. He worked with Koschützki and Meyer in Breslau and built up youth work. Recurring ill health forced him to change direction, so he started work on the journal and on publications in Stuttgart, which he could often only do from his bed. Together with pastoral work in Stuttgart, he continued this work to the end of his life. During the *Verbot* he worked at Cotta'sche Publisher, where he found hundreds of letters of Steiner's in the archives.

APPENDIX

Wilhelm Kelber, Eduard Lenz, Johannes Perthel, Husemann, Emil Bock

41. *Wilhelm Kelber*
1901 May 13, Feucht, Nürnberg
– 1967 August 27, Schwarzach im Pongau, Austria

Kelber was active in the Wandervogel with his school friend Lenz. An avid writer for the youth movement's magazine, in 1922 at university in Munich he was writing against anthroposophy when Schilling came enthusiastically to tell him about it. He made a U-turn and, together with Lenz, was at Breitbrunn. He worked in Nürnberg until 1961 when he was sent to Vienna. In 1926 he was severely ill; Ita Wegman treated him, recommending a study of Raphael's works. This led to his two-volume work on Raphael that is still in print. During the *Verbot* he was called up and at the end of the war was taken prisoner in France. He was made lenker in 1949. Overall Kelber was headstrong but always active, and he was a prolific writer.

42. *Eduard Lenz*
1901 June 18, Bad Brückenau, North Bavaria
– 1945 November 8, Omsk, Russia

With Kelber, Lenz was involved in the Wandervogel. He studied in Munich where he married Friedel Ganz. They had four children (Johannes also became a priest). He made an intensive study of anthroposophy, and was invited to the Autumn Course but declined. Just before Breitbrunn, he decided to join, saying, 'If they take someone like Willmann, I'll join.' He founded the congregation in Bochum, then worked briefly in Fürth and Hanover, before asking to join Josef Král (the first Czech priest, ordained in 1923) in Prague. Initially services were only in German (many Germans lived there), but he learned Czech, and the first Czech service was held in 1927. He became a widely travelled speaker in various congregations and at conferences. In 1934 he moved to Dresden. After the Anthroposophical Society and Waldorf schools were banned, he was involved in negotiations with the Nazi authorities to allow The Christian Community to continue. At first during the *Verbot* he worked in a paper factory, but on hearing that the Gestapo were to arrest him again for further questioning, he joined the army (where they had no jurisdiction). His two daughters died in the Dresden bombing in 1945; Lenz was captured by the Russian army at the very end of the war, and transported to Siberia. He was transported back due to ill health, but died on the train journey near Omsk.

43. *Gerhard Klein*
1902 July 7, Teplitz, Bohemia (now Teplice, Czech Republic)
– 1980 December 21, Stuttgart

Klein's father was a Lutheran minister who became acquainted with anthroposophy through Michael Bauer's daughter, and went on to become leader of the group in Mannheim, with Steiner often staying at the house. Gerhard Klein was involved in the Wandervogel, studied German at Tübingen, and was part of the founding group from the Autumn Course onwards. He first worked in Munich with Pauli and from 1924 in Dresden with Lenz. He married Elisabeth who taught at the Waldorf school there. During the *Verbot* he did agricultural work and on being called up became a medic. After the war he worked again in Munich, from 1951 in Hanover and from 1970 in Nürnberg. From there he made frequent trips to East Germany, especially Dresden. Even in later years he was always youthful. He was a storyteller, keen on drama and music.

44. *Kurt Theodor Willman*
1902 September 28, Böhstadt, Friedberg, Hesse
– 2003 May 10, Offenburg, Baden Württemberg

While studying in Marburg, Willmann went to a lecture about anthroposophy, which led to a deep connection to Steiner and to the first Goetheanum. After ordination he initially worked in Vienna, but found this difficult. News of the burning of the Goetheanum and the report of Steiner's lecture of Dec 30, 1922 by Count Polzer-Hoditz (leader of the Vienna Anthroposophical Society) led this artistic and sensitive man to a breakdown and illness. In hospital in Stuttgart Steiner declared him unable to work. In 1925 he went to Italy (largely on foot) and the following year with his wife down the Danube to Constantinople, again largely on foot. He then worked in biodynamics for the rest of his life. He was always a loner, but knew everyone and was often able to mediate in difficult situations. He was the last surviving founding priest, as he lived to be just over one hundred years old.

45. *Harald Schilling*
1902 November 21, Karlsruhe – 1943 May 11, Kalamata, Greece

Schilling grew up in Mannheim and was confirmed by Gerhard Klein's father. He studied in Kiel and, probably at Meyer's invitation, attended the Autumn Course. Aged nineteen, he was the youngest to be ordained. He started work in Kiel and married – their only daughter Sigrun was later a Community helper in Stuttgart for many years. By 1924 Schilling was burnt-out and took time off to study ancient languages in Cologne and Kiel. Initially he still worked as a priest in vacations, but less and less as time went on. By 1930 he no longer felt connected to anthroposophy. Called up during the war, he died in a plane crash in southern Greece.

Ordained on October 20, 1922
by Johannes Werner Klein in Hamburg

46. *Rudolf Meyer*
1896 February 13, Hanover – 1985 July 6, Göppingen, Baden Württemberg

Aged eighteen Meyer had appendicitis and the operation was not wholly successful. This led to him being excused from military service but also troubled his health for the rest of his life. He studied theology and philosophy at Kiel, Göttingen and Freiburg, and heard of anthroposophy from a fellow student in 1916. He was soon involved, and by 1919 was holding lectures in the north of Germany. He was involved in the founding circle from the beginning, and diligently made contact with many students prior to the founding. He was at Breitbrunn, but for some reason did not go on to Dornach, and was ordained five weeks later in Hamburg.

For many years it was said that urgent affairs of the heart made him return to Hamburg instead of going to Dornach. However, recent research into his correspondence (particularly with his mother to whom he remained very close) showed a different picture. There was a friction and even rivalry between Meyer and Bock. In 1922 Meyer was a well-travelled and experienced lecturer of anthroposophy, whereas Bock hadn't yet started lecturing. Rittelmeyer described Bock's first talks as 'outwardly awkward and faltering, inwardly dry and cooling.' Meyer was fired with the urgency of the task and keen on founding free and independent congregations. Bock (with Rittelmeyer) saw himself in the central leadership, working on more thorough preparation. In character they were opposites: Bock a fighter; Meyer seeking peace and reconciliation. Meyer, deeply affected by this conflict, stayed on in Breitbrunn. On Steiner's initiative he was called to Dornach, arriving on the evening of September 17 after all the ordinations were complete. He was at the celebration of the Act of Consecration on the following days, though it is not clear whether he took part in the rest of the course.[2]

Until the Second World War he worked in various places, always for a period of three years – first Breslau with Koschützki and Wistinghausen; then Halle; from 1928 Prague; then another stint in Breslau before Düsseldorf. In 1939 there was a deliberate attempt to strengthen the work in Switzerland before the threatening ban in Germany. For twelve years Meyer worked in Zurich, and the house The Christian Community still uses in the centre of the city was bought during this time. In 1952, following an operation for bowel cancer which paused his activity, he moved to Karlsruhe where he worked for 21 years.

Meyer was a prolific lecturer and writer, producing over forty books and several articles every year. There seemed barely any subject on which he could not write or speak!

Ordained on November 20, 1922 by Friedrich Rittelmeyer in Stuttgart

47. Hermann Heisler
1876 April 22, Mannheim – 1962 October 19, Hamburg

Heisler grew up as the second of five children in a well-to-do jeweller's family. His family wanted him to be a minister, and he studied at various universities. When his father died he inherited an eighth of the estate, and the interest from this capital enabled him to live comfortably until the hyperinflation of 1921–23. Just before becoming a trainee minister in 1899, at his brother's wedding he met a girl from Innsbruck and they instantly became engaged.

Unfortunately she was Catholic and her father forbade the marriage and any further communication. Nevertheless, two years later he heard that she was still committed to him, and in 1903 after she converted to Protestantism, they were married.

He worked in various places in Austria and Germany but was restlessly searching for deeper meaning. At the age of 35 he started reading books by Steiner which his cousin (Emil Leinhas) had given him some years earlier. He was gripped by this and gave up his ministry. He studied philosophy in Tübingen, immersed himself in anthroposophy, and soon after he met Steiner in 1913 started holding anthroposophical lectures. He was a dedicated fighter who fearlessly stated what he felt to be true and right.

In 1920 he asked Steiner to hold a course about anthroposophy and theology, to which Steiner replied that he should gather a number of written notes of interest. A year later, when he heard of a group that was interested in a renewal of religion, he did not respond, feeling that he had left the church behind. However Steiner asked Gottfried Husemann to send him a telegram to come immediately to the June Course in Stuttgart. Steiner hoped that, as a more mature and experienced minister, he would gain the respect of the younger ones.

The always diplomatic and peace-seeking Rittelmeyer, who was not at the June Course, could never see eye to eye with the tempestuous fighter in Heisler, and even Bock who was often the mediator between the older and younger ones of the group remained reserved towards Heisler.

Heisler's task was to raise funds for the new movement, and in this he was successful, even getting funding from people who had no connection to religion or to anthroposophy. Of course much of this was lost during the inflation. Before the founding, relations between Rittelmeyer and Heisler reached a nadir, and Heisler became ill. He was not at the meetings in Breitbrunn or at the founding in Dornach. Some weeks later he went to Dornach to meet Steiner, who said to him, 'Now that Geyer has dropped away, you also want to leave. Are you mad? You're not ill. Go to Stuttgart and make your peace with Rittelmeyer.' He immediately went to Stuttgart, saw Rittelmeyer, and was then ordained in November 1922.

Until the *Verbot* he worked mainly in Munich and Bavaria. After the war he was active in north Germany until his death in 1962. He was always a bit of a loner, almost an outcast. The development of The Christian Community might have been different if Geyer and Heisler had been more centrally involved.

Ordained on July 15, 1923
by Friedrich Rittelmeyer in Stuttgart

48. Karl Ludwig
**1892 October 21, Pirschen, Silesia (now Piersno, Poland) –
1931 July 2, Nürnberg**

Born into a Pietist minister's family in Silesia, Ludwig studied at five universities. While hospitalised during military service in the First World War he heard of anthroposophy. He became a Lutheran minister in Silesia, and heard Steiner lecture in Breslau in 1921. He was at the Breitbrunn meeting, but did not continue to Dornach. He was ordained nine months later. He returned to Silesia to take leave of his Lutheran congregation there. After his valedictory sermon while sitting on a coach, the horses bolted, the coach overturned and he was presumed dead. However, he recovered and took up congregational work in Nürnberg. He also ran an anthroposophical branch with Steiner's blessing. He was present at Carl Unger's (a leading anthroposophist) assassination in 1929. After five months of illness he died in 1931, the first of the founding Christian Community priests to die.

Chronology

1911	Rittelmeyer met Steiner
1917	Rittelmeyer called to the Neue Kirche in Berlin
1917 Feb 20	Steiner's lecture in Berlin with remarks about religious renewal
1920 Oct	Conference for students in Dornach when Heisler, Klein and Spörri asked Steiner about religion and anthroposophy
1921	Conference for students in Stuttgart and memorandum to Steiner
1921 June 12–16	First theological course in Stuttgart (June Course)
1921 Sep 26 –Oct 10	Second theological course in Dornach (Autumn Course)
1921 late autumn	Rittelmeyer joined circle
1922 March 5–12	Conference for students in Berlin
1922 June	Rittelmeyer resigns from Lutheran Church
1922 Aug 16 –Sep 4	Breitbrunn meeting
1922 Sep 6–22	Foundation course at Dornach
1922 Sep 16	First Act of Consecration of Man completed
1922 Dec 3 (Advent Sunday)	First public Act of Consecration

1924 Sep 5–22	Apocalypse course and pastoral-medical course
1925 Feb	Rittelmeyer appointed erzoberlenker
1925 March 30	Steiner died
1926	Bock and Krüger visited Britain
1928	Groh and Hochweber (independently) in USA
1928 Aug	Rittelmeyer at anthroposophical world conference in London
1929 Feb 4	Heidenreich moved to London
1929 June	First Act of Consecration in English in Britain
1929 Sep 24	Heidenreich married Marta Heimeran, settled in Highgate
1931 spring	House in 1001 Finchley Road bought
1931 Aug 9	Leo Baker, Oliver Mathews and Alfred Kaufmann ordained
1932	*Christian Community Journal* started
1935	Anthroposophical Society in Germany prohibited
1935 Nov 3	Adam Bittleston ordained
1938 March 23	Rittelmeyer died
1939 June 18	First ordination in Britain (Stanley Drake and Evelyn Francis in London)
1941 June	The Christian Community in Germany prohibited
1942	All priests in Britain now in London
1943 Dec	House at Glenilla Road, London, purchased
1944	Kalmia Bittleston, Eileen Hersey and Peter Roth ordained in London
1946	Albrighton Hall purchased

CHRONOLOGY

1946 July–Oct	Adam Bittleston visited North America
1947	International youth conference at Albrighton Hall
1947 Dec 7	Hegg ordained
1948	Church in Glenilla Road, London, built
1948 autumn	Hegg and Heidenreich to New York
1948 Dec 11	Founding of New York
1950 Dec 7–8	Founding of Chicago
1953	Rudolf Koehler started work in Toronto
1953	Albrighton Hall sold, Woodford House bought
1954	Botton Camphill village founded
1956	Heidenreich visited Brazil and Argentina
	Verner Hegg worked in Los Angeles and San Francisco
1959	West London congregation acquires Temple Lodge, Hammersmith
1959 Feb 15	First Act of Consecration in South Africa
1959 Dec 6	Bock died
1960	Christian Community started in South America
1961 Feb 25	First ordination in North America (Dorothy Hegg in Toronto)
1962	Oliver Mathews became lenker in Britain, Rudolf Koehler lenker in North America
1965 June 6	Christian Community started in Cape Town
1965 June 27	Christian Community founded in Johannesburg
1967	Shalesbrook (English language priest training) established
1967	First regular services in Glencraig, Northern Ireland

1968 Feb –March	Eileen Hersey's first visit to New Zealand and Australia
1969 March 11	Alfred Heidenreich died
1970–71	Carl Stegmann and others moved to California
1971 Oct–Dec	Hersey's second visit to New Zealand and Australia
1974	Michael Tapp became lenker in Britain
1974 March –April	Hersey's third visit to New Zealand and Australia
1976	Christian Community Press changed to Floris Books
1979	Michael Tapp visited Australia and New Zealand
1981	Shalesbrook closed
1986 Jan 7	Rudolf Frieling died, Taco Bay became erzoberlenker
1988 Nov 27	Christian Community founding in Australia
1989 Oct 1	Christian Community founding in New Zealand
2002 April 13	First ordination in southern hemisphere (Cheryl Nekvapil in Canberra)
2003	Chicago seminary started
2005 April 17	First Act of Consecration in the Philippines
2005	Christian Community in Ireland established in Co Clare
2011	Chicago seminary moved to Spring Valley, New York

Notes

Abbreviations used
CCJ   *Christian Community Journal*
CCN   *Christian Community Monthly Newsletter* (during wartime)
CGA   Christengemeinschaft Archiv, Berlin
GP   Heidenreich, *Growing Point*
NAm   Lewis, *Christian Community History: North America*
RB   *Rundbrief* (priests newsletter)
TF   *The Threshing Floor* (successor to CCJ from 1981)

1. Beginnings of The Christian Community in 1922

1. GP, p. 13.
2. GP, p. 15
3. *Cosmic and Human Metamorphosis*, Feb 20, 1917, pp. 42f.
4. GP, p. 27.
5. GP, p. 28.
6. Rittelmeyer, *Rudolf Steiner Enters My Life*, p. 136.
7. GP, p. 28.
8. Rittelmeyer's biography from Gädeke, *Gründer*; Wehr, *Friedrich Rittelmeyer*; Schühle, *Entscheidung*; Rittelmeyer, *Rudolf Steiner Enters my Life*.
9. GP, p. 21f.
10. Gädeke, Gründer, p. 21f.
11. Conversation with Friedwart, Bock's son, March 2010.
12. Bock, Reisetagebücher, p. 404ff.
13. Bock's biography from Gädeke, *Gründer*; Kacer-Bock, *Emil Bock*.
14. GP, p. 23f.
15. GP, p. 28f.
16. GP, p. 47f.
17. GP, pp. 29–33.
18. Steffen, *Wege der Christus-Erfahrung*, p. 21.
19. GP, p. 33f.
20. CCJ 1967, p. 21.
21. GP, p. 70.
22. GP, p. 73.
23. GP, p. 97f.
24. Huidekoper, *In silberner Finsternis*, pp. 232f.
25. CCJ 1968 Jan/Feb, p. 2.
26. Maurer, RB 237, April 1969.
27. Heidenreich's biography from Gädeke, *Gründer*; 'One Thing at a Time,' autobiographical articles in CCJ 1964–69; conversations with Michael Heidenreich and with Wolfgang Gädeke, 2014 and 2015.
28. CCJ 1965 July/Aug, pp. 77–81.
29. CCJ 1965 July/Aug, pp. 77–81.
30. Heimeran's biography from Gädeke; *Gründer*; *Marta Heimeran*; obituaries by Heidenreich, Mathews, Walsh in CCJ 1965, conversations with Michael Heidenreich and with Wolfgang Gädeke, 2014 and 2015.
31. GP, p. 67.

32 GP, pp. 77f
33 Bock, *Life & Times*, Vol. 2, p. 82.
34 Frieling's biography from Gädeke; *Gründer*; Weymann, *Im Alltäglichen*.
35 Koehler's biography from Gädeke; *Gründer*.
36 Stegmann's biography from Gädeke; *Gründer*.

2. Beginnings in Britain

1 GP, p. 95.
2 CCJ 1932 Jan, p. 23.
3 CCJ 1951, pp. 63f.
4 GP, p. 104.
5 CCN 30, 1943, p. 5.
6 Baker's biography from conversations with Michael Tapp, 2011.
7 Kaufmann's biography from conversations with Michael Tapp, 2011.
8 RB 440 1988 April, p. 3. Mathew's biography from his daughter, Jehanne Mehta (née Sylvia Mathews), written c. 1996/97, CGA.
9 GP, p. 109.
10 Gibson, *Adam Bittleston*, p. 16.
11 Gibson, *Adam Bittleston*, p. 62.
12 TF 1989 July/Aug, p. 26
13 Bittleston's biography from Robert Powell's interviews with him, NAm I, p. 44-46, and Gibson, *Adam Bittleston*.
14 TF 1986 June, p. 15.
15 Drake's biography from Tapp, RB May 1986, Walsh & Capel in TF June 1986, and comments from his daughter, Rosemary Lett.
16 Kirst, *Evelyn Francis Capel*, p. 118.
17 Kirst, *Evelyn Francis Capel*, p. 116.
18 Kirst, *Evelyn Francis Capel*, p. 124. Biography from Kirst; P Button, obituary *Guardian*, Feb 8, 2000; E.F. Capel, 'Fifty Years Ago' paper of 1989 at CGA; 'Memories of Wartime' RB 480, 1991 Dec.

3. Wartime and Postwar Years

1 Letter Heidenreich to Heimeran Oct 16, 1945.
2 Wolf-Gumpold's biography from her letter RB 1 1945; Bittleston, RB 1961.
3 RB 1, 1945, p. 7, CCN 13, p. 1.
4 TF July/Aug 1986, p. 22.
5 Eric Stadlen, TF July/Aug 1986, p. 23.
6 Hersey's biography from her autobiographical letter in RB 1, 1945; obituaries TF 1986 July/Aug; T Bay obituary CGA.
7 M Tapp, TF 1989 July/Aug, pp. 28f.
8 M Tapp, TF 1989 July/Aug, pp. 28f. Bittleston's biography from her autobiographical letter in RB 1, 1945; obituaries TF 1989 July/Aug; obituary by T. Bay, CGA.
9 *Camphill Correspondence*, Jan/Feb 1998.
10 *Camphill Correspondence*, Jan/Feb 1998.
11 Roth's biography from his autobiographical letter in RB 1, 1945; obituaries *Camphill Correspondence* 1998 Jan/Feb ; D. Ravetz in Bock, *Builders of Camphill*, pp. 165–186.
12 O. Mathews, CCJ 1962 March/April, pp. 31f.
13 Sawkins' biography from CCJ 1962 March/April, and from undated paper, probably by R. Frieling, CGA.
14 CCJ 1964 July/Aug, pp. 91f.
15 Dodwell's biography from CCJ 1964 May/June, p. 57f and July–Aug, pp. 89–93.
16 TF 1992, April/May, pp. 28f. Perkins' biography also from T. Bay, RB 1992, CGA; and K. König, *Cresset*, Easter 1963.
17 CCN 68, 1946 May, p. 5.
18 Letters Benesch and Frieling to Heidenreich, Oct 26, 1961, CGA.
19 Ravetz, *Taco Bay*, p. 42.
20 Bay's biography from Ravetz, *Taco Bay*; Lenz, *Erinnern*, Vol. 2.

NOTES

4. Expansion to America

1. NAm I, p. 287 and comments by Alice and Trauger Groh (Hermann's son) in 2016 (emailed via Oliver Steinrueck).
2. GP, p. 110f.
3. Autobiography, NAm I, p. 67.
4. Interview with Christine Issel, Sep 1988, NAm I, p. 70.
5. Hegg's biography from NAm I, pp. 50–120.
6. CCJ 1949 Jan/Feb, pp. 26f.
7. Hegg, Autobiography, NAm I, p. 100.
8. Burgevin's biography from John Hunter's notes March 30, 1990, CGA.
9. NAm I, p. 260.
10. Hunter's biography from M. Heidenreich, RB 1998, and NAm I, pp. 256–63.
11. CCJ 1950 July/Aug, p. 119.
12. Interview with Dietlind Kionke Thoemmes, NAm I, p. 151.
13. Brewer's biography from NAm I, pp. 140–67.
14. Autobiography, NAm I, p. 169.
14. Lewis's biography from NAm I, pp. 169–215.
15. RB 700, Nov 2011.
16. Brewer, 'As I Remember It,' North American Newsletter, Easter 1998, in NAm I, p. 164 (Dates in Gregg's subsequent note corrected for 1952).
17. Bergmann's biography from pre-ordination handwritten note, CGA.
18. Interview with Dietlind Kionke Thoemmes, NAm I, p. 190.
19. Email April 7, 2015.
20. RB 471, 1991 Feb, p. 5.
21. RB, 1964, p. 38.
22. RB 471, 1991 Feb, p. 6.
23. Brecker's biography from various autobiographical notes, CGA; obituaries in RB 471, 1991 Feb.

5. Southern Africa

1. Pre-ordination autobiographical sketch, CGA, quoted by Taco Bay in RB 1982 Sep.
2. Maurer's biography from South African *Christian Community Quarterly*, St John's 1983 (Heinz Maurer Memorial Issue); CCJ 1965 Sep/Oct, pp. 121–30.
3. Sleigh's biography from Sleigh, *A Walk Through my Life*; CCJ 1965 Sep/Oct, pp. 121–30.
4. Schneider, My Story, pp. 64, 111, and conversations with Michael Heidenreich, 2016.
5. Adams' biography from autobiographical notes; TF 1991 May, p. 11, and conversation with Neville Adams, 2016.

6. Australia and New Zealand

1. Handwritten autobiographical note from about 1974, CGA.
2. From obituary by Tom Ravetz which formed the basis for Tapp's biography.
3. Pecover's biography from pre-ordination autobiography, CGA; and notes from John Shaw.

7. Conclusion

1. RB 98, p. 17.

Appendix

1. Koschützki, *Fahrt ins Erdenland*, p. 306
2. Gädeke, W. *Rudolf Meyer: ein Beitrag zur Gründungsgeschichte*, with RB 2015 May.

Bibliography

Bock, Emil, *The Life and Times of Rudolf Steiner*, 2 vols. Floris Books 2008–9.
—, *Reisetagebücher*, Urachhaus, Stuttgart 1986.
Bock, Friedwart (ed.), *Builders of Camphill*, Floris Books 2004.
Francis Capel, Evelyn, *A Woman in the Priesthood*, Temple Lodge, London 1992.
Gädeke, Rudolf F., *Die Gründer der Christengemeinschaft*, Verlag am Goetheanum, 1992.
Gibson, Kenneth, *Adam Bittleston*, Floris Books 2010.
Heidenreich, Alfred, *Growing Point: The Story of the Foundation of The Christian Community*, Floris Books 1979.
Huidekoper, Ellen, *In silberner Finsternis: Eduard Lenz*, Urachhaus, Stuttgart 2013.
Hunter, John, *Just for Today: Short Meditations*, Cosmos Press, Mass. 1976.
Kacer-Bock, Gunhild, *Emil Bock: Leben und Werk*, Urachhaus, Stuttgart 1993.
Kirst, Rudolf (ed.), *Evelyn Francis Capel: A Celebration of a Pioneering Spirit*, Temple Lodge, London 1997.
Koschützki, *Fahrt ins Erdenland*, Urachhaus, Stuttgart 1940.
Lenz, Johannes, *Erinnern für die Zukunft: eine Autobiografie*, Urachhaus, Stuttgart 2002; Vol. 2, privately published.
Lewis, Richard, *Christian Community History: North America*, 3 vols. privately published 2010.
Lienhard, Pierre, *Friedrich Rittelmeyer: Témoin du Christ vivant*, Editions Iona 1998.
Marta Heimeran (privately published collection of essays in German), Christian Community, Tübingen 1965.
Ravetz, Deborah, *Taco Bay: His Life and Work*, Floris Books 2014.
Rittelmeyer, Friedrich, *Christus*, Urachhaus, Stuttgart 1936.
—, *Jesus: Ein Bild in vier Vorträgen*, Ulm 1912 (English: *Behold the Man*, Macmillan, New York 1929).
—, *Meditation: Zwölf Briefe über Selbsterziehung*, Urachhaus, Stuttgart 1929 (English: *Meditation*, Christian Community, London 1933).
—, *Meine Lebensbegegnung mit Rudolf Steiner*, Stuttgart 1928. (English: *Rudolf Steiner Enters my Life*, George Roberts, London 1929)
—, *Rudolf Steiner Enters my Life*, fifth edition, Floris Books 2013.
—, *Das Vaterunser*, Munich 1918 (English: *The Lord's Prayer*, Macmillan, New York 1931).

—, *Vom Lebenswerk Rudolf Steiners: eine Hoffnung neuer Kultur*, Munich 1921.

Schneider, Herbert Otto, *My Story*, privately printed from dictation by Bernadine Schneider, c. 2013.

Schühle, Erwin, *Entscheidung für das Christentum der Zukunft: Friedrich Rittelmeyer, Leben und Werk*, Urachhaus, Stuttgart 1969.

Sleigh, Julian, *A Walk Through my Life*, privately published South Africa, c. 2004.

Steffen, Albert, *Wege der Christus-Erfahrung*, Dornach 1991.

Steiner, Rudolf, *Cosmic and Human Metamorphosis*, SteinerBooks, USA 2012.

Wehr, Gerhard, *Friedrich Rittelmeyer: Sein Leben – Religiöse Erneuerung als Brückenshlag*, Urachhaus 1998.

Weymann, Andreas, *Im Alltäglichen das Heilige entdecken: Rudolf Frieling*, Urachhaus 2001.

Index

Italics refer to photographs, **bold** refer to longer biographies

Aaron 40
Aberdeen 91–6, 108, 113, 115, 121, *133*, 135
Act of Consecration of Man 10, 39
Adamec, Josef 93, 144, *144*
Adams, Joyce 188
Adams, Neville 48, 179, 184, *185*, **186–90**, *188*, *189*, 193, *195*, 201, 205
Adcock, Daniel 159
Adelaide 194, 200
Agricultural Course 213
Albrighton Hall 97, 108, 110, *110*
Albuquerque, New Mexico 166
Allan, Nimmo *122*
Allan, Peter 88, *122*
Allen, Muriel 113, *114*, *115*, 115f, *116*, 121, *122*, 133, 151
Allsop, Malcolm 130
'America Action' 64, 166, 168
Anthroposophical Society 21
— and The Christian Community 54, 215
—, banning in Germany 22, 30, 47
Anthroposophical World Congress (London 1928) 46, 74
Apocalypse Course 55, 210
Argentina 173
Auckland, New Zealand 194, 200
Australia 97, 124, 184, 198

Autumn Course 211

Baker, Leo 65, **70–72**, *71*, 90, 94
Balke, Paul *36f*
Ballytobin, Ireland 130
Barackman, Dorothy (married Hegg) 140
Barfield, Owen 70, 72
Barnes, Alfred and Ann 146
Baublies, Elke *122*, *202*
Bauer, Michael 19, 34, *34*, 220, 224, 226
Baumann, Paul 26
Bay, Ita (née Meeder) 124f, *125*, 127, 129, *162*, *189*, *202*
Bay, Paul 123
Bay, Taco 80, 109, *115*, 120f, *122*, **123–27**, *125*, 130, *162*, *165*, 182, *189*, *202*
Bayes, Kenneth 117
Becher, Otto 25, *36f*, 217
Beckh, Hermann 29, *36f*, 211, 213, 222
Bell, John Arthur 135
Benen House 86
Bergmann, Rosemarie 153, 156, **159–63**, *160*, *162*
Berlin 126
Besant, Annie 68
Birmingham 74, 91, 94f, 106, 113, 115, 121

INDEX

Bittleston, Adam 66, 70, **77–82,** 79, 81, 89, 91, 93, 98, 105, 113, *114, 115,* 121, 124, *128,* 129, 139–142, 163
Bittleston, Daniel 80
Bittleston, Gisela (née Hermann) 80
Bittleston, Kalmia 78, 80, 95, **98–100,** 99, 105, *114, 115, 122*
Bittleston, Stella (married East) 80
Blattmann, Fritz 36f, 215
Bock, Emil 20f, 25f, **27–31,** *28,* 32f, *36f,* 48, 66, 82, 92, 143, *143,* 147, 161, 177, 209–13, 213, 220, 223, 228f
Bock, Grete (née Seumer) 29
Boogert, Arie 200
Borchart, Martin 25, 32, *36f,* 58, 210f, 218
Borries, Hartmut *202,* 203
Boston, Massachusetts 149, 151
Botton Camphill Village 102, 108, 120, *134,* 135, 171
Botucatu, Brazil 174
Bowral, NSW, Australia 200
Boyd, Bill *122*
Bradley, Marcia *see* Dodwell, Marcia
Brangwyn, Frank 86
Brazil 173
Brecker, Walter *122, 160, 162, 165,* **169–72,** *171, 189*
Breda, Peter van *119,* 120, 186, *189,* 190
Breitbrunn 33
Brewer, Gregg 149–53, **153–56,** *155, 156,* 157, 158, *160,* 161, *162*
Brewer, Michael 155
Brewer, Natalie (née Robinson) 154, *155,* 158
Brighton 91
Bristol 70, 121, 171, 197
Buenos Aires 173

Burgevin, Frederick **147f,** *148,* 151
Burgevin, Lavinia (née Sloan) 147
Burgevin, Margaret (née Lilienfeld) 148
Button, Peter 78, 109, *115,* 121–24, *121, 133*

Cais, Louise (married Madsen) 122, 133, 135
Cali, Columbia 174
California 166
Camphill 94, 100–102, 120, 123, 151, 170, 181
Camphill School, Botswana 186
Camphill Village West Coast, South Africa 181, 183f, *183*
Canberra 200
Canterbury *134,* 135
Cape Town 175, *180,* 186
Capel, Evelyn, *see* Francis, Evelyn
Capel, Herbert 87
Capel (Surrey) 91
Chicago 126, 152, 155f, 159–161, 168
Christchurch, New Zealand 194, 200
Christian Community, The (name) 39
— and Anthroposophical Society 54, 215
—, banning of *(Verbot)* 10, 30, 52, 59, 92, 98
—, birthday 39
—, in England and America 45
Christian Community Journal 70, 93, 135, 194, 197
Christian Community Press 136
Circle of Seven 10, 126
Clanabogan 130
Clare, Co (Ireland) 131
Clayfield, Rachael (married Shepherd) 179, *180, 189*
Clement, David 78

241

Clormann, Wilhelm 25
Coffey, Kevin 200
Columbia 174
Copake Camphill village 155
Corbridge, Northumberland 121
Cresset House, South Africa 175

Dancey, Richard *160*
Davie, William *114,* 115, *115, 116, 122*
Decken, Cécile von der (née von Hodenburg) 216
Decken, Claus von der *36f,* 216
Delrow, Herts. 103
Denver 166–68, *167*
Derry, Evelyn *see* Francis, Evelyn
Derry, Samuel 86, 175
Detroit 153
Devine, Lisa *202,* 203
Devon, Pennsylvania 149, *149*
Dodwell, David 106
Dodwell, Janet (married Sharman) 108
Dodwell, Marcia (née Bradley) **106–8,** *106,* 113, *114,* 115, *115*
Doldinger, Friedrich *36f,* 212
Dostal, Jan 115, 144, *144*
Drake, Elsie (née Wright) 84
Drake, Margaret (née Gregg) 84
Drake, Rosemary (married Lett) 84
Drake, Stanley 73, 82, **83f,** *83,* 89, 93, 113, *114,* 115, *122,* 124, 127
Dreissig, Georg 184, *185*
Dresden 160
Drews, Arthur 215
Druitt, Roger *122*
Duffcarrig, Ireland 130
Duncan, British Columbia 166
Dundas, Kathleen 98
Dunshane, Ireland 130
Durban, Natal 177, 186, 190
Durham, Ontario 163

Edinburgh 80, 113, 121, 135, 146, 151
Edmonton, Canada 166
Edmunds, Francis *128*
Edwards, Irene (née Taylor) 115, 122
Edwards, Ormond *115, 118, 122, 133*
Elderton, Kathleen (married Roth) 102
Ellen, Mary 141
Ellington, Duke 145
Elmfield Rudolf Steiner School 76
Emerson College 80
Emmichoven, Willem Zeylmans van 170
Engqvist, Karl 93
erzoberlenker 10, 21
Eugene, Oregon 166

Fackler, Hermann *36f,* 215
Field, Walter Ogilvie 74, 79
Finchley Road, '1001' 70f, 82, 84
Fletcher, John 92
Floris Books 136
Forest Row 113, 124, 127, 135
Foundation The Christian Community (international) 126
Fountain, The (youth magazine) 123
France 147
Francis, Evelyn (married Derry and Capel) 82, **85–88,** *85, 87,* 90, 95, 117f, *122,* 143f, 151, 175–78, *176, 182,* 184, *185, 186, 189*
Franke, Otto 20, 25, *36f,* 221
Frankfurt, Germany 44
Freeden, Tammo von *122*
Freeman, Arnold 66
Frentzel, Jutta *36f,* 211, 223
Frieling, Margaretha (née Gayda) 59
Frieling, Rudolf 27, *36f,* 48, **56–60,** *57,* 59, 61, 124f, 147, 149, 151, 164, *176,* 211, 224

Gädeke, Wolfgang 168
Ganz, Friedel (married Lenz) 225
Gayda, Margaretha (married Frieling) 59
Gerrards Cross, Buckinghamshire 90f
Geyer, Christian 18f, *19*, 21, 32–34, 210, 213, 229
Ghana 88
Gitzke, Richard 20, 25, 29, *36f*, 217, 219f
Glas, Dr Norbert 105
Glencraig Camphill community 130
Gloucester 197
Goebel, Arnold *36f*, 221
Goetheanum, Dornach 31
Golden Blade, The (journal) 66
Golders Green, London 91
Golding, William 80
Goodall, Richard 181, *189*
Goodwin, Pearl *122*
Gradenwitz, Walter 25, *36f*, 222
Gregg, Margaret (married Drake) 84
Grimm, Werner *160, 162,* 163, *165,* 166, 201
Groh, Hermann 138, 219
Groh, Lili (née Klein) 219
Grohmann, Mechthild (married Perthel) 211
Gulbekian, Sevak 87

Habegger, Mr 173
Haes, Maarten Udo de *133,* 195
Hahn, Herbert 26
Halifax, Lord 89
Hampstead, London 91
Hapstead (Camphill) Village 109
Harwood, Cecil 67f, *69,* 79
Hawaii 166
Hawkes Bay, New Zealand 194, 200
Hawkwood College, Stroud 123
Hegg, Alstan (née Lippencott) 142, *142*

Hegg, Dorothy (née Barackman) 140
Hegg, Dorothy (née Schlie) 141–43, 165
Hegg, Evelyn 141
Hegg, Mary Ellen 141
Hegg, Verner 115, 139, **140–43,** *141, 142,* 144, *144,* 148–51, 153, 162–66, *165*
Heidenreich, Alfred 14, *36f,* 40, **41–49,** *43, 49,* 51–53, 67, *69, 71,* 74, 79, *81,* 82, 89f, 94–96, 108, 113, *114, 115,* 117f, 121, *122,* 124, 129, *129,* 135f, 138, 142–44, *143, 144,* 146f, 151f, 155, 170, 173, *176, 177,* 179, *185,* 194, 196, 212, 219, 224
Heidenreich, Michael 52, *81, 85,* 170, 196
Heimeran, Marta *36f,* 42, 44–46, **50–53,** *53,* 67, *69, 71,* 73, *81,* 89f, 95, 113, *115,* 211, 219, 224
Heisler, Hermann 22, *22,* 26f, 32, 213, 215, 222, 228
Hermann, Gisela (married Bittleston) 80
Hermanus House 175, 178
Hersey, Eileen 94, **95–97,** *96, 114, 122,* 194f, *195*
Hesse, Elisabeth (married Tapp) 196, 198
Hess, Rudolf 92
Heydrich, Reinhard 93
Hiebel, Friedrich 142
Hillcrest, Natal 191
Hindes, James *160, 162,* 166
Hinüber, Hilmar von 96
Hirschberg (?) *36f*
Hochweber, Wilhelm 138, *139,* 207
Hodenburg, Cécile von (married von der Decken) 216
Holland 65
Holman, Peter 191

Holywood, N Ireland 130
Hoppe, Elisabeth (married Hunter) 151
Huidekoper, Ellen 47
Hunt, Winifred 99
Hunter, Elisabeth (née Hoppe) 151
Hunter, John 148, 149, **150f**, *150*, 152f, 155, *160, 162*, 163, *165*, 169, 171f
Husemann, Friedrich 147
Husemann, Gottfried 22, 25, 27, 36f, 48, *143*, 211, 217, 219, 221–23, 229
hyperinflation (1922–23 in Germany) 53

Innes, Colonel 86

Jaehnig, Diethart *160, 162, 165,* 166, 168
Jeremias, Alfred 60
Jerusalem 108
Johannesburg 177
—, Lazarus Church 184, 187
Jones, Michael 78, 129
June Course 211
Junge, Hartmut 153, *160, 162,* 163

Kaltenbach, Karl 199
Kändler, Peter *115, 122,* 224
Kändler, Tom *36f,* 44, 64, 212, 223f
Karstensen, Bertha (married Koehler) 61
Kaufmann, Alfred 70, **72f**, 73, 83
Kelber, Wilhelm 36f, 42, 225
Kellenbach, Von (German consulate) 138
Kerler, Julia (married Rittelmeyer) 18
Ketel, Erin *202*
Keyserlingk, Count and Countess 33

Kiekebusch, Christoph 193
Kiekebusch's farm *192*
Kings Langley 99
Kittel, Rudolf 60
Klein, Elizabeth 226
Klein, Emma (née Krille) 210
Klein, Gerhard *36f,* 51, 213, 226f
Klein, Johannes Werner 22, *22,* 25, 27, 32, *36f,* 58, 209, 211, 218
Klein, Lili (married Groh) 219
Klockenbring, Gerard 147
Klockner, George *115, 122*
Knausenberger, Reingard *189*
Koberwitz 33
Koehler, Andreas 61
Koehler, Bertha (née Karstensen) 61
Koehler, Margaret (née Roberts) 62, 153
Koehler, Rudolf *36f,* **60–62**, *61,* 121, *128,* 129, 152f, 155, *161,* 163, 165, 171, 222
Koelln, Professor Fritz 153f, *155,* 157
Köhler, Ludwig 25, *36f,* 44, 222
König, Karl 94, 100, 108, 120, *121,* 170, 175, 182
König, Renate (married Sleigh) 175, 178, 181f
Koschützki, Rudolf von *36f,* 38, *38,* 212, 224, 228
Koschützki, Titania von 212
Kottemann, Änne 214
Kovacs, Erwin 173
Král, Josef 65, 225
Krille, Emma (married Klein) 210
Krüger, Walter 66, 67
Kurras, Eberhard 20, 25, 27, 29, *36f,* 221

Landau, Rom 141
Langbecker, James *122,* 127, *162, 165,* 171f
Lang, Erwin *36f,* 63, 220
Lauenstein, Diether 177, 193

Lazarus Church (Johannesburg) 184, 187
Leeds 73f, 80, 90–92, 94f, 98, 105, 121
Lehrs, Ernst 108, 123
Leinhas, Emil 229
Leipzig 58, 62
lenker 10
Lenz, Eduard 36f, 47, 65, 223, 225f
Lenz, Friedel (née Ganz) 225
Lenz, Johannes 225
Lett, Rosemary (née Drake) 84
Lewis, C.S. 70
Lewis, Richard 151, 153–55, *155*, **157–59**, *158, 160,* 161, *162,* 164f, *165,* 171
Lewis, Tamara (née Mangold) 159
Lilienfeld, Margaret (married Burgevin) 148
Lima (Peru) 174
Lindenmeyer, Udo 163, *176,* 179
Lippencott, Alstan (married Hegg) 142, *142*
London 70, 80, 82, 90–92, 97, 106, 117
—, 1001 Finchley Road 70, *71,* 82, 84
—, Glenilla Road 86, 95, 117f, 120
—, Hammersmith 86, 117f, *119*
—, Highgate 67f, *68*
—, Streatham 70, 91
Los Angeles 142, 159, 164, *164,* 171
Ludwig, Erk *162, 165*
Ludwig, Karl *36f*

Maclean, Christian 7, 136
MacLeod, George 94, 150
MacNeill, Duncan 151
Madsen, Jon *122*
Madsen, Louise (née Cais) *122, 133,* 135

Mangold, Tamara (married Lewis) 159
Maritz, François 193
Mathews, Inga (née Scheck) 74, 77
Mathews, Oliver 48, 50, 68, 70, *71,* **74–77,** *75,* 80, 89, 95, 98, 107, 113, *114, 115,* 121, *122,* 163, 197
Maurer, Heinz 48f, 175, *176,* **177–79,** *178,* 182, 184, *185,* 188, 191
Maurer, Liselotte (née Storr) 177f
Meebold, Alfred 215
Meeder, Ita (married Bay) 124f, 127, 129, 189, 202
Melbourne 194, 203
Meyer, Rudolf 25, *36f,* 63, 154, 157, 211, 213, 215–17, 220, 224, 227
Michael Hall School 70, 106, 113, 196
Mickisch, Waldemar *36f,* 223
Milwaukee, Wisconsin 153
Ministers' Fellowship for the Study of Rudolf Steiner 94
Mirbach, Leonore von 26
Mitchell, John 199
Mitchell, Margaret 135
Molt, Emil 14
Montreal 163
Morgenstern, Christian 34, 157
Morgenstern, Margarete 34
Moses 40
Mourne Grange, N Ireland 130
Müller, Adolf 20, 29, *36f,* 219, 223
Münzer, Horst 25

Namibia 193
Nazi regime, negotiations with 47f, 225
Nederhoed, Anke (married Roth and Weihs) 100, 102
Nekvapil, Cheryl *202,* 203f
Nekvapil, Michael *202*
Neovius, Dr 138
Netherlands 65
New School (London, later Michael Hall) 70, 106, 113, 196

Newton Dee 108, 120, 123
New York 140, 142, 145f, *145*, 155, 168, 171
New Zealand 97, 127, 184, 198
Nicholas of Cusa 148
Nielsen, Sune 204
Nike, Alice 96
Nonnenmacher, Ludwig 25
Norway 65
Nusbaum, Phillip *160, 162*, 163

Oakland, California 64, 166, 168
oberlenker 10
Ogilvie, Friedrich 142
Ogilvie, Heinrich 36f, 65, 217
Ottawa, Canada 163

Parton, Stella 87
Pastoral-Medical Course 55
Patterson, Robert 149, 151, 156, *160, 162*, 172, *176*, 179
Pauli, August 36f, 213, 226
Pecover, Rosalind 184, 194f, *199*, **200f**, *202*, 204
Perkins, Donald 94, 103, **108–10**, *109*, 113, *114*, 120, *122*, 123
Perkins, Helga (née Pfretzschner) 108, 110
Perkins, John 108
Perkins, Michael 108
Perkins, Patti 108
Perth, Australia 200
Perthel, Mechthild (née Grohmann) 211
Perthel, Johannes 36f, 58, 211
Peru 174
Pfretzschner, Helga (married Perkins) 108, 110
Philippi, Kurt 36f, 217
Philippines 184, 205
Pinkert, Violetta 220
Pohl, Kyra 194, 201
Polzer-Hoditz, Ludwig Count 227
Port Elizabeth, South Africa 175

Port Eynon, Wales 91, 135
Portland, Oregon 166
Portugal 88
Prague 65, 144
Pretoria 177, 186, 190

Raschen, Klaus 193
Raschen, Sabine 193
Ravenscroft, Trevor 181
Ravetz, Tom 102, 136, *137*, 198
Rethink conferences 168
Rittelmeyer, Friedrich 16, *17*, **18–22**, *19*, 28-30, 32f, *36f*, 39, 46f, 64, 74, 209–13, 217, 220f, 229
Rittelmeyer, Heinrich *36f*, 214
Rittelmeyer, Julia (née Kerler) 18
Roberts, Margaret (married Koehler) 62
Robinson, Natalie (married Brewer) 154f, 158
Roth, Anke (née Nederhoed) 100, 102
Roth, Kate (née Elderton) 102
Roth, Peter 95, **100–103**, *101*, *114*, *115*, 120, 130, 175, 178, 182
Rudolf Steiner College, Sacramento 64, 159
Ruhtenberg, Wilhelm 26, *36f*, 216

Sacramento, California 64, 142f, 159, 165f
Salewski, Wilhelm *36f*, 60, 216
Samson, Martin *202*, 203f
San Diego, California 166
San Francisco 64, 142, 159, 164
St Gallen, Switzerland 61
Santa Cruz, California 166
Santa Fe, New Mexico 166
Santa Rosa, California 166
Santiago, Chile 174
São Paulo, Brazil 174
Sargeant, Margaret 67f, *69*
Sargeant, Robert 67f, *69*

Satchell, Phyllis 195
Sawkins, William 94, 103, **104f,** *104,* 113
Scheck, Inga (married Mathews) 74, 77
Schickler, Wolfgang *36f,* 219
Schilling, Sigrun 227
Schilling, Harald *36f,* 63, 225, 227
Schlie, Dorothy (married Hegg) 141–43, 165
Schneider, Aenne 184
Schneider, Kurt 184, 186
Schobbert, Ute *116,* 118, *122*
Schubert, Karl 161
Seattle, Washington 166
seminary, American 126, 129, 149, 168
—, England *see* Shalesbrook
—, Hamburg 64, 126
—, Stuttgart 30, 126
Seumer, Grete (married Bock) 29
Shalesbrook 62, 80, 127–29, 132, 197, 201
Sharman, Janet (née Dodwell) 108
Shaw, George Bernard 169
Shaw, John 194, 201, *202,* 204
Sheffield 91, 105, 113, 121
Shepherd, Rachael (née Clayfield) 179, *180, 189*
Shepherd, Ven. A.P. 94
Shongweni, Natal 191
Shrewsbury, England 121
Simeon Care Home, Camphill, Aberdeen 115
Skaller, Peter 169
Sleigh, Julian 175, *176,* 177–79, **181–84,** *182, 185, 189,* 195, 205
Sleigh, Renate (née König) 175, 178, 181f
Sloan, Lavinia (married Burgevin) 147
Smit, Christian 65, 93
South Africa 102
Spiegel, Gustav *36f*

Spörri, Gertrud 22, 22, 25, 27, 29, *36f,* 52, 210, 213, 223
Spörri, Robert 25
Spring Valley, New York 140, 149, 168
St Gallen, Switzerland 61
Steffen, Albert 39f, *40*
Stegmann, Carl *36f,* **62–64,** *63, 165,* 166–68, *167,* 220
Stegmann, Christine 64
Stein, Walter Johannes 123
Steiner, Rudolf 14, *15,* 19, 20f, 26, 28, 32, 42, 45, 47, 50, 54f, 105, 143, 181, 210–13, 216, 221, 227
—, death 56
Steiner, Marie 26, 39
Steinrueck, Oliver 153
Steuck, Udo 130, *131*
Storr, Liselotte 178
Stourbridge 76, 113, *132,* 135, 171, 197
Strasbourg 147
Streatham, London 70, 91
Stroud 115, 123
Stuttgart 31, 125, 126
Stuttgart seminary 30, 126
Sullivan, Dr George Alexander 105
Sunfield Children's Home 98
Sydney 198, 200, 204
Sydow, Joachim *36f,* 222, 224

Taconic-Berkshire, New York/Mass. 149, 156
Tapp, Elisabeth (née Hesse) 196, 198
Tapp, Jonathan 197
Tapp, Michael 72, 76, 97, 115, *115, 116,* 121, *122,* 123–25, 132, 184, 195, **196–98,** *197,* 200f, *202,* 203
Tapp, Veronica 197
Taylor, Irene (married Edwards) *115, 118, 122*

Temple Lodge, London 86, 117f, *119*
Temple Lodge Publishing 118
Thackray, Douglas *122*
Theosophical Society 19
Threshing Floor, The (journal) 197
Tolkien, J.R.R 70
Toronto, Ontario 62, 163, 165
translation of rituals 67, 169, 193
Tuamgraney, Co Clare, Ireland 130, *131*

Udo de Haes, Maarten *133,* 195
Uehli, Ernst 26, 39
Ulm, Germany 51
Umlauff, Ernst 25
Unger, Carl 230
Urieli, Baruch 101, *122,* 130, *131*

Vancouver 142, 165
Verbot 10, 30, 52, 59, 92, 98
Vienna 59, 61
Villiers, Helene de *191,* 193
Voigts, Christine 193

Wahl, Ernst 27
Waldorf School 14
Walsh, Kenneth 50, 79, 82, 85f
Wandervogel (youth movement) 41f, 51

Washington D.C. 149, 166
Wegman, Ita 80, 98
Weidelehner, Helmut 211, 213
Weidelehner, Hermann 211, 213
Weihs, Anke (née Nederhoed) 100, 102
Weihs, Thomas 102
Wellington, New Zealand 194, 200
Wielki, Gisela *160, 162,* 168, *205*
Willmann, Kurt *36f,* 61, 226
Wilmot, David *122, 189,* 190f
Windhoek, Namibia 179, 190, *192,* 193
Wiser, Baroness von 113
Wiser, Gisela von *111,* 113, *122*
Wistinghausen, Kurt von *36f,* 213, 224, 228
Wolf-Gumpold, Käthe 90, **91f,** *91*
Woodford House, Keswick 111–13, 132, *111, 112*
World Congress in London 46
Wright, Elsie (married Drake) 84
Wynstones School 72

Zeist, Netherlands 218
Zeylmans van Emmichoven, Willem 170
Zurich 154, 159